CANDRAKĪRTI'S

VAJRASATTVANIṢPĀDANASŪTRA

(VAJRASATTVASĀDHANA)

SANSKRIT AND TIBETAN TEXTS

CRITICALLY EDITED

by

LUO HONG

and

TORU TOMABECHI

China Tibetology Research Center
Austrian Academy of Sciences

Sanskrit Texts from the Tibetan Autonomous Region

founded and edited in chief by

Lhagpa Phuntshogs

and

Ernst Steinkellner

No.6

中国藏学研究中心
奥地利科学院

西藏自治区梵文文本系列丛书

创办/主编

拉巴平措

及

恩斯特·斯坦因凯勒

第六卷

China Tibetology Research Center
Austrian Academy of Sciences

Candrakīrti's Vajrasattvaniṣpādanasūtra (Vajrasattvasādhana)

Sanskrit and Tibetan Texts

Critically edited

by

Luo Hong and Toru Tomabechi

CHINA TIBETOLOGY PUBLISHING HOUSE
AUSTRIAN ACADEMY OF SCIENCES PRESS
BEIJING – VIENNA 2009

Submitted to the Austrian Academy of Sciences
on October 16th, 2009,
by Ernst Steinkellner, member of the Academy

ISBN 978-3-7001-6796-9

Printed by Peking Longchang Weiye Print Ltd.

Contents

Introduction

General Remarks and Acknowledgments

1.1 General Remarks

1.1.1 Candrakīrti's *Vajrasattvaniṣpādanasūtra*

In this volume of the STTAR series, we present for the first time a Sanskrit edition, along with an edition of the Tibetan version, of the *Vajrasattvaniṣpādanasūtra* (hereafter VS) ascribed to the Buddhist Tantric author Candrakīrti. Dealing with the process of meditational realization (*sādhana*) of the state of the primordial Buddha Vajrasattva / Mahāvajradhara through maṇḍala visualization, the text is also known under the title *Vajrasattvasādhana*.[1] The VS belongs to the textual corpus of the so-called Ārya School (Tib. *'Phags lugs*) of the *Guhyasamāja* exegesis and declares its affiliation to the tradition of (Ārya-)Nāgārjuna, from whom the school's name is derived.[2]

* The present work has been sponsored by the Austrian Science Fund (FWF) in the framework of the FWF project P19862 ("Philosophische und religiöse Literatur des Buddhismus"). We sincerely acknowledge the generous support we have received from the Fund.

[1] The Tibetan translation of the VS bears the title *rDo rje sems dpa'i sgrub thabs* / *Vajrasattvasādhana*. This latter title is also used by Indian authors, such as Muniśrībhadra, when referring to the VS. Cf. Muniśrībhadra, *Pañcakramaṭippaṇī Yogimanoharā*, 6a4 (Jiang and Tomabechi 1996: 11): *ācāryacandrakīrtikṛtavajrasattvasādhanābhiprāyam ādāya...*

[2] See below, Sanskrit text p. 4: *imam arthavaśaṃ jñātvā mayā śrīnāgārjunapādaparamparayā samājavyākhyātantrānusāreṇa* .... As far as we know, however, no Sanskrit equivalent of the Tibetan expression *'Phags lugs* has been attested in Indian works. It should therefore be

The author, Candrakīrti, is almost certainly not the same person as the famous seventh century Mādhyamika who wrote such works as the *Prasannapadā* and *Madhyamakāvatāra*, though Indo-Tibetan tradition usually does not differentiate between the Mādhyamika Candrakīrti and his Tāntrika namesake. As the foundation of the Ārya School should be placed not earlier than the late eighth century,[3] the VS can hardly be attributed to the Mādhyamika author. On the other hand, the author of the VS seems to be the same Candrakīrti as the one who wrote an important commentary on the *Guhyasamājatantra*, i.e., the *Pradīpoddyotana* (PU). Both the VS and PU belong to the corpus of the Ārya School. Furthermore, in the PU Candrakīrti appears to mention the VS as his earlier work.[4]

As is well known, the meditational systems of the late-period Buddhist Tantras generally consist of two different types of procedures, namely the Steps of Generation (*utpattikrama*) and the Steps of Completion (*niṣpannakrama/utpannakrama*).[5] The VS, along with the *Piṇḍīkrama* ascribed to Nāgārjuna as well as Nāgabuddhi's *Vyavastholi*, expounds the Steps of Generation of the Ārya School. As the full title of the text, *Śrī-*

noted that expressions such as "Ārya School," "Ārya Tradition," etc., are just convenient labels with little grounding in the Indian tradition.

3 For a discussion concerning the foundation of the Ārya School, see Tomabechi 2008.

4 PU 27,8 (Chakravarti 1984): *sarveṣām āsanādiniyamaḥ sādhanopayikāyāṃ kṛta eva* |. Here, the *Sādhanopayikā* is very probably an alternative title of the VS. The formulation "*kṛta eva*" suggests that this passage refers to a previous work of the author himself.

5 Cf., for example, *Guhyasamājatantra* 18.84 (Matsunaga 1978: 119): *kramadvayam upāśritya vajriṇāṃ tatra deśanā* | *kramam autpattikaṃ caiva kramam autpannakaṃ tathā* ||; *Pañcakrama* 1.2 (Mimaki and Tomabechi 1994: 1): *utpattikramasaṃsthānāṃ niṣpannakramakāṅkṣiṇām* | *upāyaś caiṣa sambuddhaiḥ sopānam iva nirmitaḥ* ||; *Hevajratantra* 1.8.25 (Tripathi and Negi 2001: 87): *kramadvayaṃ samāśritya vajriṇā dharmadeśanā* | *utpattibhāgaṃ kathitam utpannaṃ kathayāmy aham* ||.

guhyasamājamahāyogatantre bhavotpattikrameṇa vajrasattvaniṣpādanasūtram, indicates, the *utpattikrama* meditation expounded in the VS is essentially a symbolic process of the birth (*bhavotpatti*) of deities from the sexo-yogic union between the practitioner and his yogic consort. In the next section, we shall present an overview of the contents of the VS.

1.1.2 A Synoptic Analysis of the VS

General outline: The meditational procedure expounded in the VS is structured in the "standard" manner of *utpattikrama*, that is, following the three-fold *samādhi*-system. Following the introduction (**I**) and the preparatory process (**II**), the practitioner first realizes his own benefit (*svārtha*) by becoming the central deity of the maṇḍala by means of a process called *samādhirājāgrīsamādhi* or *ādiyogasamādhi* (**III**). This latter step comprises four sub-steps: *yoga*, *anuyoga*, *atiyoga* and *mahāyoga*. Through these four steps, the triple body of the Buddha, i.e., *dharma°*, *sambhoga°* and *nirmāṇakāya*, is accomplished and the practitioner himself becomes a Buddha. In the next step, *maṇḍalarājāgrīsamādhi* (**IV**), the practitioner emanates—gives birth to—the deities of the *Guhyasamājamaṇḍala* by means of a sexo-yogic union with his consort (*mudrā*). See below, pp. xxxii–xxxiii, for the arrangement of the *Guhyasamāja* 32-deity maṇḍala and the list of maṇḍala deities. The deities thus created then act for the benefit of other beings (*parārtha*). The third and last *samādhi* is called the *karmarājāgrīsamādhi* (**V**). Though called a *samādhi*, it mainly concerns various prescriptions regarding the daily activities of a practitioner such as sleeping, eating, etc., as well as miscellaneous rites (*karman*).

Below is a synopsis of the contents of the VS (between the square brackets are page-line references to our Sanskrit and Tibetan editions):

II.5 Visualization of the grounds and palace

II.5.1 Visualization of the grounds (*bhūbhāga*) [Skt. 9,9 / Tib. 41,13]

II.5.2 Visualization of the palace (*kūṭāgāra*) [Skt. 10,6 / Tib. 42,8]

III Samādhirājāgrī(*alias* Ādiyoga)samādhi

III.1 Yoga – Realization of Emptiness/*dharmakāya*

III.1.1 Visualization of the sādhaka's own self as the blue Mahāvajradhara
[Skt. 11,4 / Tib. 43,10]

III.1.2 Emanation of maṇḍala deities (visualisation of the *bāhyamaṇḍala*)
[Skt. 11,9 / Tib. 43,18]

III.1.3 Retraction of the maṇḍala deities into the sādhaka's body (*kāyamaṇḍala*)
[Skt. 12,13 / Tib. 45,3]

III.1.4 Placement of maṇḍala deities on aggregates, elements and sense faculties; dissolution of deities into Emptiness
[Skt. 14,8 / Tib. 46,17]

III.1.5 Emerging from Emptiness as Vajrasattva
[Skt. 15,3 / Tib. 47,11]

III.2 Anuyoga – Visualization of the self as the white Mahāvajradhara (*sambhogakāya*)
[Skt.15,14 / Tib. 48,7]

III.3 Atiyoga – Accomplishment of the self as *nirmāṇakāya*

III.3.1 Placement of five Buddhas on the aggregates (*skandha*)
[Skt. 16,8 / Tib. 49,4]

III.3.2 Placement of four goddesses on the elements (*dhātu*)
[Skt. 17,4 / Tib. 49,15]

III.3.3 Placement of eight Bodhisattvas on the sense faculties (*āyatana*), etc.
[Skt. 17,8 / Tib. 50,2]

V Karmarājāgrīsamādhi

V.1 Subtle yoga (*sūkṣmayoga*), recitation (*jāpa*), re-entering into Thusness (*tathatā*) and awakening by four goddesses
[Skt. 28,14 / Tib. 62,18]

V.2 Praise by Tathāgatas
[Skt. 30,7 / Tib. 64,5]

V.3 Concluding process (*upasaṃhāra*) of meditation
[Skt. 31,8 / Tib. 65,11]

V.4 Auxiliary rites
[Skt. 32,3 / Tib. 66,4]

1.1.3 Commentaries and Related Texts

The Tibetan Tanjur preserves the following two commentaries on the VS:

- The ***Vajrasattvasādhananibandha / rDo rje sems dpa'i sgrub thabs kyi 'grel pa*** (D 1815, *rGyud*, *ṅi*, 204b6–209a3; P 2679, *rGyud 'grel*, *gi*, 178a2–182b3) is a work by **Līlāvajra**, who is said to have been one of the twelve (or ten, if Buddhaśrījñāna and Dīpaṅkarabhadra are not counted) successive Vajrācāryas of Vikramaśīla. He was probably active during the first half of the 11th century.[6] This commentary was translated into Tibetan by Bu ston Rin chen grub (1290–1364). Though currently not yet available to us, a Sanskrit manuscript that is very possibly of this commentary was reported by Rāhula Sāṅkṛ-

6 On the succession of Vajrācāryas of Vikramaśīla, see Sanderson 2009: 158ff.

tyāyana among his findings at Źwa lu Ri phug, the hermitage of Bu ston.[7]

- The ***Vajrasattvasādhanabhāṣya / rDo rje sems dpa'i sgrub pa'i thabs kyi bśad pa*** (D 1835, *rGyud*, *ci* 280b2–285b4; P 2704, *rGyud 'grel*, *ṅi*, 380b7–387a5) is a work of **Tathāgatarakṣita**, the translator of the VS itself into Tibetan.[8] The commentary was translated into Tibetan by Dīpaṅkararakṣita and Khams pa Ba ri, who also revised Tathāgatarakṣita's translation of the VS. No Sanskrit original of this commentary is known to us. This commentary mainly focuses on the explanation of the passages that Candrakīrti quotes from the *Guhyasamājatantra*.

Besides the commentaries, the following two texts are worth mentioning as being closely related to the VS:

7 See Sāṅkṛtyāyana 1938: 145. According to Sāṅkṛtyāyana's description, the manuscript is complete and consists of four folios. It was copied by Vibhūticandra, one of the nine minor *paṇḍita*s who accompanied the famous *mahāpaṇḍita* Śākyaśrībhadra into exil in Tibet at the beginning of the 13th century. In fact, Bu ston says in the colophon to his Tibetan translation that he translated the text using Vibhūticandra's manuscript (P182a6–7: *bi bhu ti tsandra'i rgya dpe la bltas nas | dge sloṅ rin chen grub kyis | dpa' bo'i lo smin drug can gyi zla ba'i tshes ñer bźi la bsgyur ba'o ||*).

Wang Sen's (王森) list of the Sanskrit manuscripts in the Library of National Minorities (民族圖書館藏梵文貝葉經目録, 1985; reprinted in Hu-von Hinüber 2006) also includes Līlāvajra's *Vajrasattvasādhana*, which is probably the same manuscript as the one reported by Sāṅkṛtyāyana (according to Wang Sen, however, the manuscript consists of fourteen, rather than four, folios; the discrepancy may be due to Wang Sen's overlooking that other texts are contained in the same bundle). The former collection of the Library of National Minorities is now being examined by Professor Duan Qing (段晴), *et al.*, at Peking University. It is hoped that details about the manuscript in question will be made available in the near future.

8 See the colophon to the Tibetan translation, pp. 66–67 below.

- An **anonymous text** in Ms. Göttingen Xc 14/30b(1)[9] quotes extensively from the VS. We collected these quotaions and present them in Appendix 1 to this volume. We also made use of it as a secondary textual witness for editing the Sanskrit text of the VS. Though this is an anonymous text and its title is unknown, we use the abbreviation "**VNU***" for the sake of convenience (this text is a secondary redaction based on another collection of quotations called the *Vajrācāryanayottama*). For this material, see below 2.3.1.

- A text called the ***Mantroddhāra***[10] contained in Ms. Göttingen Xc 14/30a is a short work that is essentially a list of the *mantra*s which have been extracted (*ud-*$\sqrt{}$*dhṛ*) from the VS. The colophon ascribes it to the same author as that of the VS, i.e. Candrakīrti. This text also serves as a succinct topical outline of the meditational process expounded in the VS. We present an edition of the *Mantroddhāra* as Appendix 2 to this volume.[11] For details about this manuscript, see 2.1.3 and 2.3.2 below.

---

9 This text is basically a collection of quotations from several works belonging to the Ārya School. For an general introduction to this text, see TOMABECHI 2004.

10 The full title of the work is *Śrīguhyasamājamahāyogatantre bhavotpattikramasādhanasya mantroddhāraḥ*. See Appendix 2, p. 92 below

11 The opening passage of the *Mantroddhāra* is appended to the colophon of the Tibetan translation of Līlāvajra's *Vajrasattvasādhananibandha* (P182a7–b2): *sṅags kyi ṅes pa daṅ po ste || gñis pa dgod pa bstan pa 'o || rnam par bźag pa yaṅ gsum ste || bźi pa de ñid bstan pa 'o || źes pa sgrub thabs kyi go rims te | 'di'i don ni daṅ por sṅags kyi tshig sgrub thabs las phyuṅ nas sems kyi kun tu brtags pa ṅes par 'gyur ro || de nas phuṅ po la sogs pa rnams su rnam par snaṅ mdzad la sogs pa'i rnam pas dgod pa'o || bkod pa'i lha rnams re re'i mthar gyis raṅ gi mtshan ñid yoṅs su śes śiṅ ṅes par rtogs pa'i lha'i 'khor lo'o || phra mo'i rnal 'byor gyis gcig tu byas nas rab tu źugs te gnas pa las laṅs te | ṅes par byuṅ ba'i sṅags las dgod par 'gyur ro || źes so || ṅes pa'i sṅags ni badzra dhṛk hūṃ oṃ sumbha źes pa la sogs pa'o || 'di 'aṅ sṅar gyi rgya dpe'i rjes su byuṅ ṅo || ||*. See and compare Appendix 2 below.

1.2 Acknowledgments

The present work would have been impossible to complete, if it were not for the initiative and help of many people and institutions, to whom we would like to express here our sincere gratitude. First of all, we would like to thank Professor Lhagpa Phuntshogs, Director General of the China Tibetology Research Center (CTRC), and Professor Ernst Steinkellner, the former Director of the Institute for the Intellectual and Cultural History of Asia, Austrian Academy of Sciences (IKGA). The fruitful collaboration between our two institutes for the study of precious manuscript materials that are preserved in the TAR has been made possible by their strong initiative. Professor Steinkellner also took the trouble to read the first draft edition together with us and offered many useful comments and improvement to it.

Our thanks also go to the colleagues in Beijing, Vienna and Japan. Professor Dramdul, Director of the Institute for the Study of Religion at the CTRC, provided access to the Center's resources and ideal conditions for the collaboration between the two editors of this volume. Cynthia Peck-Kubaczek, secretary at the IKGA, kindly checked and improved our English. Dr. Kano Kazuo, Koyasan University, organized a three-day reading session during Tomabechi's visit to Koyasan in November 2008. Our edition of the Sanskrit text benefited considerably from the comments and remarks provided by the participants of the session. We would like to express our gratitude to those who participated in the reading session—to Professor Fujita Kōkan, Professor Okuyama Naoji, Dr. Tanemura Ryūgen, Mr. Ōmi Jishō, Mr. Nishiyama Kendai, Mrs. Shinoda Junko, and the graduate students of Koyasan University.

Last but not least, we would like to thank heartily two leading specialists in the area of Tantric Buddhism. Professor Harunaga Isaacson, Hamburg, and Professor Francesco Sferra, Naples, read our manuscript carefully and helped us to improve it by providing a number of useful comments.

* * *

We are grateful to all the above-mentioned people and institutions, whose invaluable help enabled us to complete this volume. If the present work proves to have any scholarly merit, the credit must belong to them. That said, all the errors and shortcomings in this book are, of course, exclusively our own responsibility.

October 2009

Luo Hong (Beijing)

Toru Tomabechi (Vienna)

Source Materials

2.1 Sanskrit Manuscripts

For the present edition of the VS, we have consulted three Sanskrit manuscripts, **A**, **B**, and **G**, as primary textual witnesses. As we had access to the codices only through photo-reproductions, we had to rely on Luo Zhao's (罗炤) unpublished catalogue[12] (for Mss. A and B) and Rāhula Sāṅkṛtyāyana's report on his first expedition to Tibet in 1934[13] (for Ms. G) for the descriptions of manuscripts' physical features.

2.1.1 Manuscript A

The photostat copy that we have used of Manuscript A is stored as pp. 38/9-41 in Box 77 of the Sanskrit manuscript collection kept at the China Tibetology Research Center (CTRC) in Beijing and is registered on p. 57 in Sandak's (gSaṅ bdag) unpublished list of microfilms kept at the CTRC (中国藏学研究中心收藏的梵文贝叶经(缩微胶卷)目录). In Luo Zhao's catalogue, this manuscript is described on pp. 166–167 of the section on the Potala palace collection.

This incomplete manuscript preserves five palm-leaf folios

12 On this catalogue, see Steinkellner 2004: 21–23; Steinkellner 2007: xii–xiii, n. 5. Luo Zhao's descriptive catalogue of the Sanskrit manuscript in the TAR comprises two major parts, one being the section on the Nor bu gliṅ ka collection (罗布林卡所藏贝叶经目录, 1984) and the other on the Potala palace collection (布达拉宫所藏贝叶经目录, 1985).

13 Sāṅkṛtyāyana 1935.

(fols. 2–6) out of six, with the first folio being lost. According to Luo Zhao's description, the folio-size is 61.1cm by 5.9cm. Except for folio 6b, which contains four lines, the text is written in six lines on both sides of the folios. Each text line contains approximately 140 *akṣara*s. Two string holes with surrounding blank space divides each folio into three equal blocks of text, and each block is further delimited by vertical lines across the folio to ensure that the layout is consistent. As for the Sanskrit pagination, only "*dvi*" as a letter-numeral on the left-hand margin of folio 2b is visible. Since the right-hand margins of the folios are broken off, it is possible that the original pagination was found on the right-hand margins and that the pagination on the left-hand margins was secondary. Tibetan pagination in *dbu can* script has been added to the left-hand margin of the recto of each folio.

The manuscript is written in hook-topped Nepalese script. The type of script is similar to that in Mss. Bendall Add. 1686 and Add. 1691.2 in the Cambridge collection. The latter two are dated respectively to 1165 CE and 1179 CE[14] and our Manuscript A belongs very probably to the same period, i.e. around the second half the 12th century.

On the upper left margin of folio 2a, the following Tibetan line in *dbu med* is found:

> *dpal gsaṅ ba 'dus pa'i skyed rim rdor sems bsgrub pa ẓla ba grags pas mdẓad pa'o* ||

The colophon of the manuscript (6b2–3) reads as follows:

> *śrīguhyasamājamahāyogatantre bhavotpattikrameṇa vajrasatvaniṣpādanasūtraṃ samāptam*|| || *kṛti⊙r iyaṃ candrakīrtteḥ*|| *250* ||

[14] See BENDALL 1883, PLATES II.3, III.1 and "Table of Letters."

After the colophon, a summary ("*saṃgrahasūtra*") of the VS is found:

> (6b3) *idānīṃ saṃkṣepeṇa saṃgrahasūtram āha | prathaman tāvat* sthānaniyamaḥ karuṇālamba⊙naṃ śūnyatālambanaṃ bhūtaniṣpādanaṃ | kūṭāgāramaṇḍalavinyāsaḥ paramārthaḥ praveśaḥ vyutthānasūryā*(6b4)*lambana| paryante candramaṇḍalaṃ vajradharaniṣpādanaṃ | mantrādhiṣṭhānena skandhādyāpūraṇakāyavākci⊙ttādhiṣṭhānaṃ | maṇḍalotsargaḥ | sūkṣmayogaḥ | vajrajāpaḥ vāg*va'jāpaḥ | paramārthapraviṣṭasaṃcodanaṃ | punarvyu⊙tthānastutikaraṇaṃ | upasaṃhāraḥ karmmaprasarāntas tato valo'ddhavyam iti || sūtramelāpaka(ṃ)* ||

This summary is found neither in Mss B, G nor in the Tibetan translation.

2.1.2 Manuscript B

The photostat copy of Manuscript B is stored as pp. 24/5-28 in Box 122 of the Sanskrit manuscript collection at the CTRC and is registered on p. 103 of Sandak's list. Luo Zhao describes this manuscript on pp. 34–35 of the Potala palace section of his catalogue.

This manuscript, which must have consisted of thirteen folios, lacks its first leaf[15] and thus twelve folios (fols. 2–13) have been preserved. The material is palm-leaf and the folio-size, according to Luo Zhao's report, is 30.7cm by 5.2cm. The text is written in six lines on both sides of the folios, except for 13b,

---

15 A Tibetan note referring to the loss of the first folio is found on the right bottom corner of folio 13b: *rnal 'byor chen po'i rgyud gsaṅ ba'i dam tshig(?) gi cho ga dbu nas śog bu 1 chad.*

which contains only five lines. A string hole, which is slightly to the left of the center, is punched into each folio. A blank space surrounds the string hole, covering an area that is equivalent to five *akṣaras* horizontally and three lines vertically. The script used in this manuscript is Proto-Bengali.

The colophon includes the date of the manuscript, the scribe's name and the original owner of the book:

> (13b3) *śrīguhyasamājamahāyogatantre bhavotpattikrameṇa vajrasa*(13b4)*tvaniṣpādanasūtraṃ samāptaṃ* || || *granthasya pramāṇaṃ sapā⊙daśatadvayam** || *śrīmadbhojavarmmadevapādīyasamvat 17 sūryage? kārttikadine 15* || *likhitam idaṃ pustakaṃ* || || *kāyasthasambhaladevena* || *pustikeyaṃ paṇḍit{i}avibhūtiśriyaḥ* ||[16]
>
> The *sūtra* on the accomplishment of Vajrasattva through the process of birth, related to the glorious *Guhyasamājamahāyogatantra*, is finished. The length of the text is two-hundred and a quarter (i.e. 250 = 200 + 200 × 1/4) [*śloka*s]. On Sunday (?, *sūryage*), the 15th day of the *Kārttika* month in the 17th regnal year of the glorious Bhojavarman, the book was copied by the professional scribe Sambhaladeva. This book belongs to the scholar Vibhūtiśrī.

The date given here, however, is problematic, since the reign of Bhojavarman in North India lasted only 4 years, from ca. 1285 to 1288 CE.[17] Ḥammīravarman,[18] his successor, ascended the throne in 1288 and ruled till 1311 CE. A possible explanation is that Bhojavarman's regnal years continued to be counted during the reign of his successor.[19] If such is the case, the 17th

16 This colophon is accompanied by a transcription in Tibetan letters that is added below each line.

17 Cf. Dikshit 1976: 173.

18 Cf. Dikshit 1976: 176–177.

19 For such practices, see Salomon 1998: 172.

regnal year of Bhojavarman would correspond to 1301 CE. As for the scribe, Sambhaladeva, and the owner of the manuscript, Vibhūtiśrī, we have little clue to their identity.

2.1.3 Manuscript G

Manuscript G is the only complete codex of the VS known to us. It is actually a part of a longer palm-leaf manuscript in which at least ten Tantric works related to the Ārya School of the *Guhyasamāja* exegesis are consecutively copied. There, the VS is included as the second item and it occupies six and a half folios (13b3–19a2). The manuscript was photographed by Rāhula Sāṅkṛtyāyana in 1934 at Ṅor Monastery.[20] Positive prints were later brought to Göttingen along with other materials photographed by Sāṅkṛtyāyana, and these are now in the custody of the Niedersächsische Staats- und Universitätsbibliothek, Göttingen. The prints of our Manuscript G is registered there under shelfmark Xc 14/30a.[21]

According to Sāṅkṛtyāyana's report, the folio-size is 12 1/3 by 2 1/6 inches (ca. 31.5cm by 5.5cm). The texts are written in nine lines on both sides of the folios in Proto-Bengali script. A short decorated Tibetan line, "*zla grags kyi rdo rje sems dpa'i sgrub thabs*," is found in the upper margin of folio 13b, just above the beginning of the VS.

The internal colophon to the VS (19a2) reads as follows:

> *śrīguhyasamājamahāyogataṃtre bhavotpattikrameṇa vajrasatva-niṣpādanasūtraṃ samāptaṃ || kṛtir ācāryacandrakīrttipādānām*

[20] See SĀṄKṚTYĀYANA 1935: 36. In Sāṅkṛtyāyana's list, the manuscript-bundle is numbered as Ṅor XVIII and is reported as containing eight texts.

[21] See BANDURSKI 1994: 66–68; TOMABECHI 2004: 40–41; TOMABECHI 2006: 18; KANO 2005: 141–142.

iti || granthapramāṇaṃ 250 ||

The final colophon of the entire manuscript having been lost, no information on the date, the name of scribe, etc., is available. It may however be possible to assume, on palaeographical grounds, that this manuscript was probably copied sometime around the 12th–13th centuries.

2.2 Tibetan Translation

The VS was first translated into Tibetan by Tathāgatarakṣita and Klog skẏa gŹon nu 'bar at the Vikramaśīla monastery. Later, the translation was revised by Dīpaṅkararakṣita and Khams pa Ba ri at the dPe med lhun grub temple of Tho liṅ / mTho ldiṅ monastery.[22] It is to the latter revised version that we have access through the Tibetan Tanjur. For our edition of the Tibetan text, we collated the following four exemplars:[23]

D = sDe dge No. 1814, *rGyud, ṅi* 195b6–204b6
[*The sDe-dge Bstan-'gyur*, Delhi: Karmapae Chodhey Gyalwae Sungrab Partun Khang, 1982–1985]

N = sNar thaṅ No. 677, *rGyud, gi* 166a7–176a6
[Scanned image "W22704-3287-eBook.pdf," New York: Tibetan Buddhist Resource Center]

22 See the colophon to the Tibetan text below. Cf. also the colophon to Tathāgatarakṣita's commentary, P387a5: *tho liṅ dpal dpe med lhun gyis grub pa'i gtsug lag khaṅ du rgya gar gyi mkhan po mkhas pa chen po dī paṃ ka ra ra kṣi ta daṅ khams ba ri lo tsā bas bsgyur ba'o* ||.

23 We excluded the Co ne edition from our collation, as this edition, being a virtual copy of D, is known to be of little value as an independent testimony.

P = Peking No. 2678, *rGyud 'grel, gi* 168b2–178a2
[*The Tibetan Tripitaka. Peking Edition—kept in the Library of the Otani University, Kyoto—, Reprinted under the Supervision of the Otani University, Kyoto*, Tokyo-Kyoto: Tibetan Tripitaka Research Institute, 1955–1961]

S = "Golden Manuscript" No. 681, *rGyud 'grel, gi* 217b1–230a5
[Scanned image "W23702-1024-eBook.pdf," New York: Tibetan Buddhist Resource Center]

2.3 Source Materials for Appendices

2.3.1 Appendix 1

Appendix 1, a collection of the passages of the VS quoted in an anonymous text (VNU*), is based on a Sanskrit manuscript found in the bundle shelved as Xc 14/30b at the Niedersächsische Staats- und Universitätsbibliothek, Göttingen.[24] The VNU* is the first item of the bundle, which contains three manuscripts. These manuscripts were photographed by Rāhula Sāṅkṛtyāyana at Ṅor monastery, but are not mentioned in his reports about his expeditions to Tibet. The manuscript consists of fifty-nine palm-leaf folios and is complete. The text is written in five lines on both sides of the folios and is in Bengali script of the 12–13th century.

[24] On this manuscript, see Bandurski 1994: 67; Tomabechi 2004: 41–42; Kano 2005: 141–142.

2.3.2 Appendix 2

Appendix 2, an edition of the *Mantroddhāra*, is based on the same manuscript as G (see above 2.1.3), and we use the same siglum. The location of the text in the manuscript is 27b2–29a2.

Editorial Policy, Signs, and Abbreviations

3.1 Editorial Policy

3.1.1 Sanskrit text

General editorial policy: The three codices of the VS we have consulted are apparently of mutually independent transmissions. Quite often they present three different but equivalent readings (such as *svabhāva* vs. *svarūpa* vs. *rūpa*) which makes choosing quite problematic. In such difficult cases, we *tentatively* give preference to the reading in Ms. G, whose readings generally make better sense and are relatively consistent. Where no satisfactory reading can be found among the codices, we propose emendations based on secondary witnesses. In this latter case, larger weight has been given, in principle, to the Tibetan translation than to others.

Apparatus: Our Sanskrit edition has two types of apparatus. The first reports testimonia (citations in/from other texts, etc.). To indicate the different types of testimonia, we have adopted the system proposed in Steinkellner 1988 (e.g. Ce = *citatum ex alio* for citation from another text, etc.; see below, list of abbreviations).

The second, critical apparatus, is positive. The accepted readings and variants are separated by means of colons (:) and multiple variants are separated by semicolons (;). Supporting evidence, where deemed necessary, is given in parentheses just after the accepted reading. Where a non-trivial variation among the manuscripts occurs or where we have proposed an emendation, we have indicated this by printing the footnote in boldface and marking the location in the text with a star (⋆). Other footnotes are printed in normal typeface and marked with an asterisk (*).

Sandhi, *anusvāra* and punctuation: The classical rules of sandhi are silently applied throughout the text. The use of *anusvāra* has been standardized in the following manner: (1) *anusvāra* is used only at word-endings or before *y, r, l, v, ś, ṣ, s* and *h*; (2) the so-called pseudo-*anusvāra* has been replaced with the corresponding class nasal. Punctuation is entirely editorial and the original punctuation of the manuscript is not reported in the critical appratus.

3.1.2 Tibetan text

General editorial policy: The variation among the four exemplars we collated is relatively small. Where a variation occurs, the reading of D is generally preferred, as it as a rule presents gramatically correct forms and/or corresponds better to the Sanskrit text.

Apparatus: The critical apparatus is positive. The accepted readings and variants are separated by colons (:) and multiple variants are separated by semicolons (;).

Punctuation and orthography: Punctuation is entirely editorial and we do not report variations in the use of *śad*, etc. in the different exemplars. Words in abbreviated form (*bsdus yig, bskuṅs yig*) are reported in their normalized form in the apparatus without reporting the original form.

3.2 Editorial Signs and Abbreviations

The following signs are used for the critical apparatus (Sanskrit and Tibetan texts).

3.2.1 Editorial Signs

•	illegible part(s) of an *akṣara*
••	illegible *akṣara*
///	broken / damaged part of the manuscript
*	*virāma* (explicitly written)
0	*virāma* (implied)
’	*avagraha*
‹ ›	contain *akṣara*(s) added in the manuscript
( )	contain unclear *akṣara*(s) or unclear parts of an *akṣara*
?	uncertain reading
!	sic
{ }	contain *akṣara*(s) cancelled by means of dots
⦃ ⦄	contain *akṣara*(s) cancelled by means of erasure
< >	contain emendational additions
⊙	string-hole
×	blank space in the manuscript (approximately equivalent to one *akṣara*)
|	*daṇḍa* / *śad*

|| double *daṇḍa* / *ñis śad*
¦ line-filling sign (broken or crossed *daṇḍa*)
+ line-filling sign (§-shaped mark)

3.2.2 Abbreviations

A	Ms. A of the CTRC collection
add.	added in
B	Ms. B of the CTRC collection
Ce	*citatum ex alio* = citation from another text
Cee	*citatum ex alio modo edendi* = citation from another text, with redactional changes
Ci'e	*citatum in alio usus secundarii modo edendi* = citation in another text, with redactional changes, not marked as a citation
CMP	*Caryāmelāpakapradīpa* (ed. WEDEMEYER 2007)
D	sDe dge edition of the Tibetan Canon
em.	emended
G	Ms. Göttingen Xc 14/30a
GST	*Guhyasamājatantra* (ed. MATSUNAGA 1978)
Ms(s)	manuscript(s)
n.e.	no equivalent in
N	sNar thaṅ edition of the Tibetan Canon
om.	omitted in
P	Peking edition of the Tibetan Canon
Pi	*Piṇḍīkrama* (ed. TRIPATHI 2001)
PK	*Pañcakrama* (ed. MIMAKI and TOMABECHI 1994)

PU	*Pradīpoddyotana* (ed. CHAKRAVARTI 1984)
S	"Golden Manuscript" Tanjur
SBS	*Sarvabuddhasamāyogaḍākinījālasaṃvara* (Tib. P No. 8, *rGyud*, *ka* 164a5–209a2)
SRT	*Sarvarahasyatantra* (ed. WAYMAN 1984)
SVT	*Sandhyāvyākaraṇatantra* (Tib. P No. 83, *rGyud*, *ca* 238b2–290b1)
T	Tibetan text of the VS
TD	Tibetan text of the VS (sDe dge)
TP	Tibetan text of the VS (Peking) (as edited in this volume)
VNU*	anonymous text in Göttingen Xc 14/30b (see above, p. xvii)
VS	*Vajrasattvaniṣpādanasūtra*
YM	*Pañcakramaṭippaṇī Yogimanoharā* (ed. JIANG and TOMABECHI 1996)

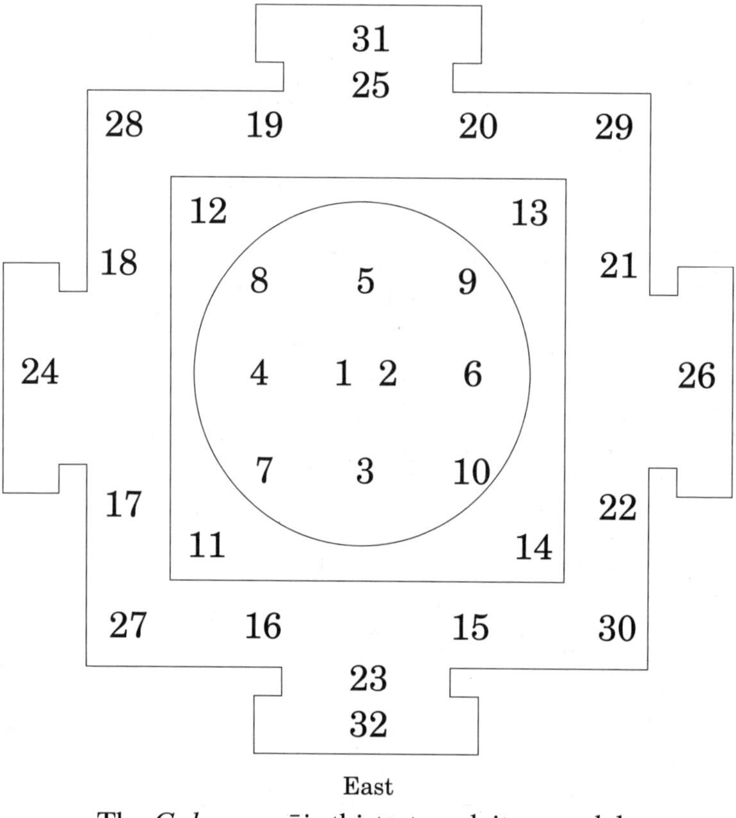

The *Guhyasamāja* thirty-two deity maṇḍala

	Deity	*bīja*	Placement
1.	Akṣobhya	HŪṂ	heart / consciousness (*vijñānaskandha*)
2.	Sparśavajrā	—	tactile object (*sparśaviṣaya*)
3.	Vairocana	OṂ	head / matter (*rūpaskandha*)
4.	Ratnasambhava	SVĀ	navel / sensation (*vedanāskandha*)
5.	Amitābha	ĀḤ	throat / figuration (*sañjñāskandha*)
6.	Amoghasiddhi	HĀ	feet / volition (*saṃskāraskandha*)
7.	Locanā	MOHARATI	earth (*pṛthivīdhātu*)
8.	Māmakī	DVEṢARATI	water (*abdhātu*)
9.	Pāṇḍaravāsinī	RĀGARATI	fire (*tejodhātu*)
10.	Tārā	VAJRARATI	wind (*vāyudhātu*)
11.	Rūpavajrā	—	visual object (*rūpaviṣaya*)
12.	Śabdavajrā	—	sound (*śabdaviṣaya*)
13.	Gandhavajrā	—	smell (*gandhaviṣaya*)
14.	Rasavajrā	—	flavor (*rasaviṣaya*)
15.	Maitreya	MAIṂ	tendon (*snāyu*)
16.	Kṣitigarbha	THLĪṂ	visual faculty (*cakṣurāyatana*)
17.	Vajrapāṇi	OṂ	audio faculty (*śrotrāyatana*)
18.	Ākāśagarbha	OṂ	olfactory faculty (*ghrāṇāyatana*)
19.	Lokeśvara	OṂ	gustatory faculty (*jihvāyatana*)
20.	Mañjuśrī	HŪṂ	mental faculty (*manaāyatana*)
21.	Sarvanivaraṇaviṣkambhin	OṂ	tactile faculty (*kāyāyatana*)
22.	Samantabhadra	SAṂ	joints (*śarīrasandhi*)
23.	Yamāntaka	HŪṂ	right hand (*dakṣiṇabhuja*)
	Vajravetālī*	—	right hand
24.	Aparājita	HŪṂ	left hand (*vāmabhuja*)
	Aparājitā*	—	left hand
25.	Hayagrīva	HŪṂ	mouth (*mukha*)
	Bhṛkuṭī	—	mouth
26.	Amṛtakuṇḍali	HŪṂ	genitals (*guhya*)
	Ekajaṭā*	—	genitals
27.	Acala	HŪṂ	right arm (*dakṣiṇabāhu*)
	Viśvavajrī*	—	right arm
28.	Ṭakkirāja	HŪṂ	left arm (*vāmabāhu*)
	Viśvaratnī*	—	left arm
29.	Nīladaṇḍa	HŪṂ	right knee (*dakṣiṇajānu*)
	Viśvapadmī*	—	right knee
30.	Mahābala	HŪṂ	left knee (*vāmajānu*)
	Viśvakarmī*	—	left knee
31.	Uṣṇīṣacakravartin	HŪṂ	head (*mūrdhan*)
	Gaganavajriṇī*	—	head
32.	Nisumbharāja	HŪṂ	feet (*pāda*)
	Dharaṇīndharī*	—	feet

List of thirty-two maṇḍala deities and ten female fierce deities

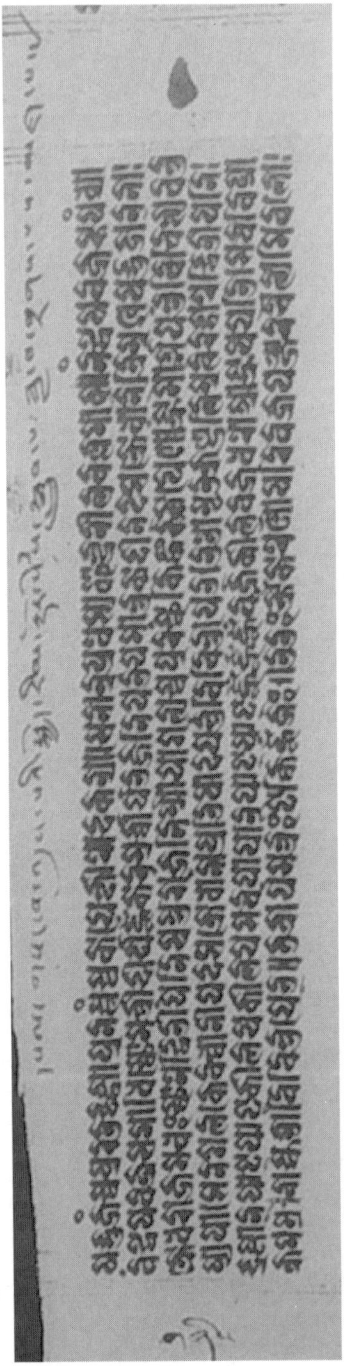

Ms. A, folio 2a (left third)

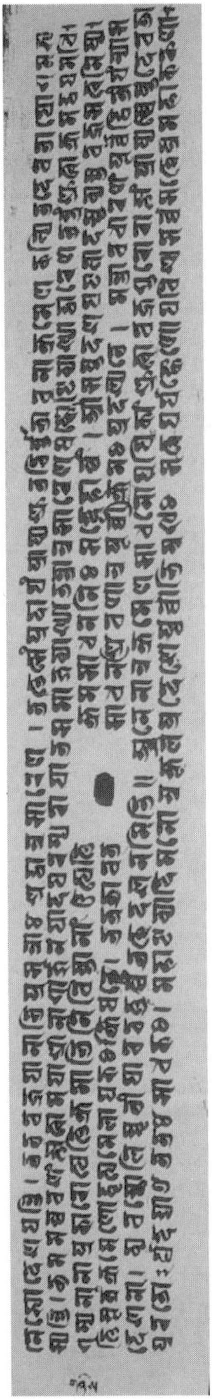

Ms. B, folio 2a

Sanskrit Text

नमो वज्रसत्त्वाय॥ G13b3
G3

[I.1] बुद्धयानाभिसमयगोत्राः प्रावचनिकाः कल्याणमित्रप्रसङ्गाद्वज्रयान- TD195b6 TP168b4
मारुह्य कल्पितदेवतायोगसमाधिसमापन्नाः [a] षट्कोटिव्याख्याबहिर्मुखा
G4
वज्राचार्यमाराध्य यथारुतशब्दार्थद्वारेण श्रीगुह्यसमाजमहायोगतन्त्रं
श्रुत्वा बालप्रबोधनार्थं तन्त्रादुद्धृत्य यथाप्राप्तोपदेशानुसारेण कल्पितदे-
G5
वतायोगस्य नानाशब्दरचनाविशेषेण साधनाङ्गान्यपि कुर्वन्ति ॥

[I.2] तत्र केचिद्वज्राचार्याश्चन्द्रवज्रक्रमेण वज्रसत्त्वनिष्पत्तिं कल्पयन्ति । TD196a2 TP168b6
केचिद्भवोत्पत्तिक्रमेण । केचित्पञ्चाकाराभिसम्बोधिक्रमेण । केचि-
G6
ज्झटितिक्रमेण वज्रसत्त्वनिष्पत्तिं कल्पयन्ति ॥[a]

माण्डलेयदेवतास्तु केचित्त्रयोदशेच्छन्ति । केचिदूनविंशति। केचि- TD196a3 TP168b7
त्पञ्चविंशतिदेवतान्यासमिच्छन्ति ॥
G7

एवमस्मिन्तन्त्रे नानाकारणमाश्रित्य वज्रसत्त्वादिदेवतामूर्तिं निष्पाद- TD196a4 TP168b8
यन्ति । तदनुसारेणापि टीकां पञ्जिकां च कृत्वा विनेयजनेभ्यो देश- B2a
B1
यन्ति ॥

---

[a] **Cf.** PU 228,21–24

---

1 dpal 'jam pa'i rdo rje la phyag 'tshal lo T instead of namo vajrasattvāya **2** gsuṅ rab 'chad pa'i dge ba'i bśes gñen T for prāvacanikāḥ kalyāṇamitra° **3** devatā n.e. T ○ °**samāpannāḥ** em. : °**samāpannān*** G **4** kha phyir bltas pa'i rdo rje slob dpon T for °bahirmukhā vajrācāryam **6** °viśeṣeṇa sādhanāṅgāny api em. : °viśeṣeṇa? sādhanāṅgāny a?pi G (cf. sadbhāvatantrād uddhṛtya bālaprabodhanārthaṃ sādhanāṅgāni pradīpakāni kriyante CMP 337,7–8); sgrub thabs la sogs pa … khyad par gyis (em. : khyad par gyi TD, khyad kyis TP) luṅ rjes su byed do T **7** vajra n.e. T **8** ākāra n.e. T **9** skad cig bźi'i T for jhaṭiti ○ niṣpatti n.e. T **10** **kecit** em. : **kvacit** G ○ 'dod do add. T **12** °kār{e}aṇam G **13** 'grel bśad daṅ | dka' 'grel la sogs pa T for ṭīkāṃ pañjikāṃ ca

TD196a5 TP169a1 तत्र वज्रयानाभिप्रसन्नाः श्रद्धानुसारेण तत्तत्सम्प्रदायं प्राप्य श्रुतचिन्ता-भावनाक्रमेण कल्पितदेवतायोगमभ्यस्यन्ति ॥

TD196a6 TP169a2 [I.3] इममर्थवशं ज्ञात्वा मया श्रीनागार्जुनपादपरम्परया समाजव्याख्या-तन्त्रानुसारेण षट्कोटिव्याख्याद्वारेण तन्त्रं श्रुत्वा क्रमद्वयमधिगम्य नानाप्रकारोत्पत्तिक्रमाभिनिविष्टानामुत्पत्तिक्रमसाधननिःसन्देहार्थम् आ सप्तदशपटलादस्तव्यस्तवज्रसत्त्वनिष्पत्तिसूत्रं क्रमेणोद्धृत्य मेलापकः G14a क्रियते ॥

TD196b1 TP169a4 [II.1] [b] तत्र तावत्साधनश्रवणानुपूर्वीक्रमः प्रदर्श्यते —

मन्त्रावधारणं पूर्वं द्वितीयं न्यासदेशना ।
व्यवस्थोलिस्तृतीया तु चतुर्थं तत्त्वदर्शनम् ॥

इत्यनेनानुक्रमेण साधनोपयिकां श्रुत्वा वज्रगुरोराज्ञां प्राप्य स्वेष्टदेवतायाः पुरतो ऽर्घं दद्यात् । ततः साधको महाटव्यादिमनोऽनुकूलप्रदेशे पूर्वाभिमुखः सत्त्वपर्यङ्केणोपविश्य सर्वसत्त्वेषु म-

---

[b] **Ci'e** VNU* 5b3–6a1

---

1 de kho na ñid kyi T for tattat 2 °kramena ⋯⋯yogam G 3 mayā B : m{ā}ayā G ◦ 'phags pa dpal T for śrī ◦ **paraṃparayā** G (brgyud pa las T) : **paramparāyāta°** B (āyāta n.e. T) ◦ **samāja°** B : **śrīsamāja°** G (śrī n.e. T) 4 °vyākhyādvāreṇa B : °⋯reṇa G 5 °otpattikramābhiniviṣṭānāṃ B : °otpa˙i⋯⋯ G ◦ utpatti° B : ⋯tpatti° G; utpatti n.e. T 6 asta° B : a‹sta›° G ◦ astavyasta n.e. T ◦ rdo rje sems dpa' bskyed pa nas le'u bcu bdun pa la thug pa mdo T for ā saptadaśapaṭalād astavyastavajrasattvaniṣpattisūtram 8 **sādhanaśravaṇānupūrvī°** G : **sādhana{śravaṇānupūrvvī}°** B; śravaṇa n.e. T 10 **tu** G : **ca** B 11 °opayikāṃ B (cf. PU 27,8) : °opāyikāṃ G 12 °**devatāyāḥ** em. : °**devatāyā**? G; °**devatā°** B 13 °**manonukūlapradeśe** em. (yid daṅ rjes su mthun pa'i gnas su T) : °**manonukūle pradeśe** B : °**mano'nukūle** G

हाकरुणाचित्तमुत्पाद्य स्वपरहितहेतोर्वक्ष्यमाणक्रमेण वज्रसत्त्वपदं सा- B2b
धयेत्[b]। अस्य सूत्रं द्वादशपटले —

[c]महाटवीप्रदेशेषु फलपुष्पाद्यलङ्कृते ।
पर्वते विजने साध्यं सर्वसिद्धिसमुच्चयम्[c] ॥

इति ॥

[II.2] [d]तदनन्तरं साधकः शून्यताधिमोक्षेण प्राकृताहङ्कारमपनीय झ- TD196b4 TP169a8
टित्यात्मानं महावज्रधररूपं शुक्लवर्णमधिमुञ्चेत्[d]। अस्य सूत्रं तृती-
यपटले —

[e]आकाशधातुमध्यस्थं भावयेद्बुद्धमण्डलम् ।
रश्मिमेघमहाव्यूहं बुद्धज्वालासमप्रभम्[e] ॥

इति ॥

[II.3] [f]ततः प्रथमपटलोक्तज्ञानप्रदीपवज्रसमाधिन्यायेन [g]वज्रधृगिति[g] म- TD196b5 TP169b2
न्त्रमुच्चार्य तेनाक्षोभ्यरूपं कृष्णवर्णं त्रिमुखं षड्भुजमात्मपुरःस्थं दृ- A2a
ष्ट्वा पुनस्तं स्वकाये क्षीरोदकन्यायेनानुप्रवेश्येन्द्रनीलवर्णमात्मानं द्वे-

---

[c] **Ce** GST 12.2 [d] **Ci'e** VNU* 7b3–5 [e] **Ce** GST 3.1 [f] **Ci'e** VNU* 7b5–8a3 [g] **Ce** GST 6,22

---

1 svaparahita° G : svaparihata[!]° B ○ vakṣyamāṇa° G : vakṣamāṇa° B ○ bdag daṅ gźan la phan pa'i rdo rje sems dpa'i go 'phaṅ T for svaparahitahetor ... vajrasattvapadaṃ 2 don T for sūtra 7 jhaṭity G : sa[!]ṭity B ○ **mahāvajradhara**° B (rdo rje 'chaṅ chen po'i T) : **vajradhara**° G 13 tenā° G; te{ta}nā° B ○ **ātmapura<ḥ>sthaṃ** em. (bdag ñid kyi mdun du T) : **ātmapura[!]sthaṃ** G; **svapurata**[!] A; **svapura[!]{¨}‹sthaṃ›** B 14 punas tam n.e. T ○ °**nyāyenā**° BG (tshul gyis T) : °**nyāsenā**° A ○ **indranīlavarṇṇam** AB (indra nīla'i mdog can T) : **indranīlam** G

षवज्ररूपं ध्यायात् । [f] अस्य सूत्रं प्रथमपटले — [h] सर्वतथागतकायवाक्चित्तविद्यापुरुषो ऽक्षोभ्यमहामुद्रासंयोगपरमपदेन कृष्णसितरक्ताकारेण सर्वतथागतकायवाक्चित्तवज्रस्य सर्वतथागतकायवाक्चित्तवज्रे निषीदयामासेति [h] ॥

TD197a1 TP169b5 B3a [II.4.1] [i] एवं द्वेषवज्रसमाधिस्थो मन्त्री दीर्घहूंकारमुच्चार्य तज्जनितयमान्तकादिदशक्रोधान् त्रिमुखषड्भुजान् नानाप्रहरणव्यग्रहस्तान् दशदिग्व्यवस्थितान् दुष्टतर्जनतत्परान् विचिन्तयेत् [i] । अस्य सूत्रं त्रयोदशपटले —

[j] क्रोधा द्वेषालये जाता नित्यं मारणतत्पराः ।
सिध्यन्ति मारणार्थेन साधकस्याग्रधर्मिणः [j] ॥

इति ॥

TD197a3 TP169b7 [II.4.2] [k] ततो निसुम्भराजमधःस्थाने द्वितीयं निसुम्भराजं निर्मायागत्य स्वपुरःस्थं किङ्कररूपेणाज्ञां मार्गयन्तं विचिन्त्य चतुर्दशपट-

---

[h] **Cee** GST 6,23–25 [i] **Ci'e** VNU* 8a3–4 [j] **Cee** GST 13.27 [k] **Ci'e** VNU* 8a4–b1

---

2 °**padena** BG (go 'phaṅ T) : °**deśanā** A **3** °**cittavajrasya** AG (thugs rdo rje'i T) : °**cittasya** B **4** °vajre AB : ˙˙˙˙ G **5** evaṃ BG : /// vaṃ A ○ dveṣavajra° AG : dveṣavajr{e}a° B ○ °**stho** AB (gnas nas T; VNU*) : °**samāpanno** G ○ **mantrī** AB (sṅags pas T; VNU*) : **vajrī** G ○ **tajjanita**° BG (de bskyed pa'i T; VNU*; YM) : **tajjaniyata**° A **6** °**ādi**° BG (VNU*) : °**ādīn*** A ○ °praharaṇa° BG : praharaṇāṃ! A **7** °tarjjana° AB : °ta˙˙˙˙° G ○ **vicintayet** AB : **cintayet** G **12** **nisumbha**° B : **niśumbha**° G; **ni///krodha**° A (krodha n.e. T) ○ nisumbha° AB : niśumbha° G **13** **svapura<ḥ>**° em. : **svapura**° ABG ○ kiṅkara° AB : ˙iṅkara° G ○ gnod mdzes kyi gzugs kyis T for kiṅkararūpeṇa

लोक्तचतुर्हूंकारमन्त्रेणाज्ञां दद्यात् । तत्रायं मन्त्रः — ओं सुम्भ निसुम्भ हूं गृह्ण गृह्ण हूं गृह्णापय गृह्णापय हूं आनय हो भगवन्विद्याराज हूं फट् ॥

[II.4.3] ततो निसुम्भराजं दशदिशो गत्वा देवादिविघ्नाधिपती- TD197a4 TP170a1 G14b
नङ्कुशेनाकृष्य पाशेन गलके बद्ध्वानीय दशक्रोधानां प्रतिपादयन्तं विचिन्तयेत् । ततो ऽमृतकुण्डलिमुत्तरद्वारे द्वितीयनिर्माणं संस्थाप्यात्मानं दशकीलरूपाकारमभिनिर्माय दशविघ्नाधिपतीनां शिरसि B3b
निपतितं विचिन्तयेत् । ततो निसुम्भराजं व्युत्थाय वज्रमुद्गरेण मन्त्रमावर्त्याकोटयन्तं ध्यायात् । तत्रायं मन्त्रः — ओं घ घ घ घ घातय घातय सर्वदुष्टान् फट् फट् कीलय कीलय सर्वपापान् फट् फट् हूं हूं हूं वज्रकील वज्रधरो आज्ञापयति । सर्वविघ्नानां काय-

---

[l] **Ce** GST 65,16–17 [m] **Ci'e** VNU* 8b1–2 [n] **Ci'e** VNU* 9b3–10a2 [o] **Cee** GST 69,9–10

---

2 sumbha nisumbha AB : śumbha niśumbha G ○ **ho** B (T; GST) : **hoḥ** AG (cf. hoḥ VNU*) **4** nisumbha° AB : niśumbha° G ○ **daśadiśo** AG : **daśadig** B **5** **aṅkuśenā°** BG : **ā'ṃkuśen///°** A ○ °ākṛṣya G : °///ṣya A; °ākṛ‹śya'› B ○ **baddhvā°** AG (bciṅs nas T) : **baddhā°** B **6** 'mṛtakuṇḍalim AG : amṛtakuṇḍal{ī}‹i›m B ○ **dvitīya°** AB : **dvitīye** G **7** **daśakīlarūpākāram** A : **¨śak{i}‹ī›laka|rūpākāram** B; **daśakīlakāraṃ'm** G (rūpa n.e. T) ○ **°ādhipatīnāṃ** A : **°ādhipatīna'ṃ** G; **°adhipatīn** B **8** nisumbha° AB : niśumbha° G **9** **gha gha gha gha** B; **gha 4** G (VNU*, YM) : **gha gha** A; gha gha T for gha gha gha gha **10** ghātaya AG : ghāta{ka}‹ya› B ○ hūṃ hūṃ add. T **11** **phaṭ phaṭ hūṃ hūṃ hūṃ** A : **phaṭ phaṭ hūṃ hūṃ** BG; hūṃ hūṃ phaṭ phaṭ | hūṃ hūṃ hūṃ T for phaṭ phaṭ hūṃ hūṃ hūṃ ○ ba dzra kī la ya T for vajrakīla ○ ājñāpayati AG : a'jñāpayati B ○ sarba duṣṭāṃ bi ghnāṃ T for sarvavighnānām

वाक्चित्तवज्रं कीलय हूं हूं फट् फट् । अस्य सूत्रं त्रयोदशपटले—

[p] वज्रामृतमहाक्रोधं वज्रकीलं विभावयेत् ।
निखनेद्[G4]दशदिशाग्रे [B4] तु स्फुलिङ्गज्वालसुप्रभम् [p] ॥

इति ॥

TD197b1 TP170a5 [II.4.4] [q] ततष्टक्किराजमन्त्रेण लोहजलाग्निवायुप्राकारचतुष्टयं यथाक्रमं बाह्यतो विचिन्तयेत् । तत्रायं मन्त्रः — [r] [B5] टक्कि हूं [r] जः। [A6] ततो भ्रूंकारेणोपरि वज्रपञ्जरं [G5] चैत्यमिव लोहप्राकारोपरि व्यवस्थितम्' [B6] त्र्यक्षरेण च कवचम्' हूंकारेण विश्ववज्रमयं भूभागं विचिन्तयेत् [q] ॥

TD197b2 TP170a7 B4a [II.4.5] एवं दिक्सीमाबन्धवज्रप्राकारपञ्जरादिविधिपूर्वकं रक्षाचक्रं [B1] ध्यायात् । अस्यानुशंसासूत्रं [G6] त्रयोदशपटले —

---

p **Cee** GST13.79 q **Ci'e** VNU* 10a3–5 r **Ce** GST 64,21

---

1 °**cittavajraṃ** G; °**cittava‹jraṃ›** B (GST) : °**cittaṃ** A; tsitta badzra T for cittavajraṃ ○ **kīlaya** AG (T) : **kīlaya ‹2›** B ○ **hūṃ hūṃ phaṭ**⁰ **2** B; **hūṃ 2 phaṭ**⁰ **2** G (VNU*) : **hūṃ phaṭ*** A; hūṃ phaṭ T for hūṃ hūṃ phaṭ phaṭ ○ trayodaśa° BG : daśon!daśa A 3 °**krodhaṃ** AG (khro bo T) : °**rājaṃ** B ○ **vibhāvayet** BG : **prabhāvayet** A (rab tu bsgom T) 4 nikhaned BG : nikhane! A; spro bar bya T for nikhanet ○ **daśadiśāgre tu** B : **daśadiśāgre** G; **daśadiṅmaṇḍalāgre** A 6 °**prākāra**° AB (ra ba T) : °**prakāra**° G 7 **ṭakki** AG : **ṭākki** B 8 hūṃ T for bhrūṃ ○ °pañjaraṃ BG : °pañjara! A 9 **tryakṣareṇa ca kavacaṃ|| hūṃkāreṇa viśvavajramayaṃ bhūbhāgaṃ** A (yi ge gsum gyis go cha la'o || hūṃ gis sa'i cha la sna tshogs rdo rje'i rang bzhin du T) : **hūṃkāreṇa viśvavajramayaṃ bhūbhāgaṃ tryakṣareṇa kavacaṃ** B; **hūṃkāreṇa viśvavajramayaṃ bhūbhāgaṃ tryakṣaramantreṇa kavacaṃ** G 10 °**‹vajra›prākāra**° A (rdo rje'i ra ba T) : °**prākāra**° BG ○ °**pūrvakaṃ** AB : °**pūrvaka**° G 11 °ānuśaṃsā° AG : °ānusa!ṃsā° B

ध्यानजेन समादानं यत्र स्थाने समाचरेत् । A2b
अनेन ध्यानयोगेन तिष्ठन्बुद्धैरधिष्ठ्यते ॥

इति ॥

[II.4.6] ततो द्वितीयपटलोक्तया बोधिचित्तगाथया रक्षाचक्रं त्रैधातुकं च TD197b3 TP170a8
तथतायां प्रवेशयेत् । तत्रेयं गाथा —

अभावे भावनाऽभावो भावना नैव भावना ।
इति भावो न भावः स्याद्भावना नोपलभ्यते ॥

इति । इयमपि परमा रक्षा ॥

[II.5.1] तत आकाशधातुमध्ये यंकारेण धन्वाकृति वायुमण्डलं TD197b5 TP170b2
हूंकारद्वयेन पार्श्वयोर्वज्रद्वयाङ्कितं विचिन्त्य' तदुपरि रंकारेण त्रिकोणाग्निमण्डलं वज्रद्वयाङ्कितम्' पुनस्तदुपरि वंकारेण वर्तुलं वारुणमण्डलं वज्रद्वयाङ्कितं विभाव्य' तदुपरि लंकारेण चतुरस्रं माहे-

---

[s] **Cee** GST 13.78 [t] **Ci'e** VNU* 10b2–4 [u] **Ce** GST 2.3 [v] **Ci'e** VNU* 10b4–11a1

---

1 bsam gtan gaṅ gis yi dam ni T for dhyānajena samādānam 2 **adhiṣṭhyate** G; **adhiṣṭhyata** B : **adhiṣṭhita** A 4 °**paṭaloktayā** G : °**paṭalokta**° A; °**paṭalo‹kta›**° B ○ °**gāthayā** BG : °**gāthāyā** A 6 bsgom par bya ba sgom pa med T for bhāvanā naiva bhāvanā 7 dṅos daṅ dṅos med pa'i T for bhāvo na bhāvaḥ syāt 8 don dam pa'i T for paramā 9 **tata** AG : om. B ○ **yaṅkāreṇa** A; **yaṃkāreṇa** B : **yaṃkārajaṃ** G ○ °**ākṛti** AG : °**ākṛtiṃ** B ○ vāyumaṇḍalaṃ BG : ///maṇḍala! A 10 **vajradvayāṅkitaṃ** AG (rdo rje gñis kyis T) : **vajrāṅkitaṃ** B 11 trikoṇāgni° AG : trikoṇ{o}āgni° B ○ °dvayā° BG : °dvay{o}ā° A ○ punar n.e. T ○ vartulaṃ AB : vartulaṃm! G 12 **vāruṇa**° AG : **varuṇa**° B ○ **vibhāvya** AG : om. B (vibhāvya n.e. T) ○ caturasraṃ BG : catusra!ṃ A

न्द्रमण्डलं वज्रद्वयाङ्कितं विभाव्य। मण्डलचतुष्टयं संहृत्य पृथिवीमण्डलमात्रं ध्यायात् । अस्य सूत्रमेकादशपटले —

खवज्रमध्यगतं चिन्तेन्मण्डलं सर्ववज्रजम् ।
G15a भ्रूंकारं भावयेत्तत्र वज्रमेघसमावहम् ॥

इति ॥

TD197b7 TP170b5 B4b [II.5.2] एवमाधारमण्डलं निष्पाद्य भ्रूंकारेण कूटागारम्

चतुरस्रं चतुर्द्वारं चतुस्तोरणशोभितम् ।
चतुःसूत्रसमायुक्तमष्टस्तम्भोपशोभितम् ॥

हारार्धहाररचितं मणिवज्रार्धचन्द्रकम् ।
खचितं वज्ररत्नैस्तु द्वारनिर्यूहसन्धिषु ॥

कुम्भस्तम्भमहावज्रं क्रमशीर्षस्तु पक्षिणी।
घण्टापताकसंशोभं चामरादिविभूषितम् ॥

इति । अस्य सूत्रमष्टमपटले —

W **Cee** GST 11.3   X **Ci'e** VNU* 11a1–3

---

3 nam mkha'i khams T for khavajra ○ khavajramadhyagataṃ BG : /// vajra{dvaya}madhyagataṃ A ○ pāda a hypermetric 4 mñam 'phro'o T for samāvaha (cf. vajrameghaspharāvaham GST) 6 bźi add. TP 7 °**śobhitaṃ** AG : °**bhūṣitaṃ** B 8 thig le T for sūtra 10 tu BG : tur! A 11 **kumbha**° AG (bum pa T) : **aṣṭa**° B ○ **pakṣiṇī** BG (bya can T) : **pakṣiṇi** A 12 ldan pa T for saṃśobha 13 iti n.e. T

[y] योजनशतविस्तारं चतुरस्रं सुशोभनम् ।
चतूरत्नमयं चैत्यं स्वच्छं प्रकृतिनिर्मलम् ॥ [y]

इति ॥

[III.1.1] [z] एवङ्गुणविशिष्टं देवमनुष्यातिक्रान्तं प्रासादवरं पृथिवीमण्डलो- TD198a3 TP170b8 परि विचिन्त्य चन्द्रसूर्याद्यासनं संस्थाप्य स्वयं प्राकृताहङ्कारमपनीय झटिति महावज्रधररूपमात्मानमिन्द्रनीलवर्णं त्रिमुखं षड्भुजं दक्षिणे वज्रं चक्रं पद्मं वामे घण्टां चिन्तामणिं खड्गं सम्पुटयोगेन मध्यमण्डले पद्मचन्द्रासने सत्त्वपर्यङ्केणोपविष्टं विचिन्तयेत् ॥ [z] B5a

[III.1.2] ततः पूर्वे वैरोचनम्' दक्षिणे रत्नसम्भवम्' पश्चिमे ऽमि- TD198a5 TP171a3 ताभम्' उत्तरे ऽमोघसिद्धिम्' अग्निकोणे लोचनाम्' नैर्ऋत्यां मामकीम्' वायव्यां पाण्डरवासिनीम्' ऐशान्यां तारां गर्भमण्डले प्रविचिन्त्य' द्वितीयपुटे ऽग्निकोणे रूपवज्राम्' नैर्ऋत्यां शब्दवज्राम्' वायव्यां गन्धवज्राम्' ऐशान्यां रसवज्राम्' मध्ये स्पर्शवज्रां व-

---

[y] **Cee** GST 8.18 [z] **Ci'e** VNU* 11a3–b1

---

1 **suśobhanaṃ** AG : **suśobhaṃ‹›** B 2 catū° G : catu° AB 4 **prāsādavaraṃ** BG (VNU*) : **prāsādaṃ varaṃ** A 5 °**āsanaṃ** AG (gdan T; VNU*) : °**ā‹›** B 6 **mahāvajradhararūpam** A (rdo rje 'chaṅ chen po'i gzugs T; VNU*) : **mahāvajradharam** B; **mahāvajrarūpam** G ○ **dakṣiṇe** A (g-yas kyis T; VNU*) : om. BG 7 **vajraṃ cakraṃ padmaṃ** AG (rdo rje daṅ 'khor lo daṅ padma T; VNU*) : **cakraṃ padmaṃ ‹vajraṃ›** B ○ **vāme** AB : **saṃyuktena**? **vāmena** G (saṃyukta n.e. T) ○ dkyil 'khor gyi dbus su T for madhyamaṇḍale 8 °paryaṅkeṇo° BG : °paryaṅkeno!° A ○ °opaviṣṭaṃ AG : °opapa!viṣṭaṃ B ○ **vicintaye**t* B; **vicintayet*** G (VNU*) : **cintayet*** A 10 nairṛtyāṃ BG; nai///tyāṃ A 12 **śabdavajrāṃ** BG : **śabdavajrā** A 13 **vāyavyāṃ gandhavajrāṃ aiśānyāṃ rasavajrāṃ** G; **‹¨yavyāṃ gandhava¨ ¨śānyāṃ rasavajrām*›** B : **pā!yavyāṃ gandhavajrāṃ aiśānyāṃ rasavajrāṃ** A

ज्रसत्त्वं समालिङ्ग्य स्थितां चिन्तयेत् । तथा तृतीये पुटे पूर्वप-
A3a ट्टिकायां मैत्रेयं क्षितिगर्भम्' दक्षिणपट्टिकायां वज्रपाणिं खगर्भम्'
पश्चिमपट्टिकायां लोकेश्वरं [B4] मञ्जुघोषम्' उत्तरपट्टिकायां [A1] सर्वनिवर-
णविष्कम्भिणं समन्तभद्रम्' पूर्वद्वारे यमान्तकम्' [G7] दक्षिणद्वारे ऽप-
राजितम्' पश्चिम[B5]द्वारे हयग्रीवम्' उत्तरद्वारे ऽमृतकुण्डलिम्'
अग्निकोणे ऽचलम्' नैर्ऋत्यां टक्किराजम्' वायव्यां नीलदण्डम्'
ऐशान्यां महाबलम्'[G8] ऊर्ध्वमुष्[B6]णीषचक्रवर्तिनम्' अधो निसुम्भराजं[A2]
ध्यायात् । अस्य सूत्रं <u>प्रथमपटले</u> —

B5b [a]स्वच्छं च तत्स्वभावं च नानारूपं समन्ततः ।
[B1]बुद्धमेघसमाकीर्णं स्फुलिङ्गगहनाकुलम् ।
स्वच्छादिमण्डलैर्युक्तं सर्वताथागतं पुरम् ॥[a]

इति ॥

TD198b3 TP171b1 [III.1.3] एवं बाह्यमण्डले[B2] द्वात्रिंशद्देवतानिर्माणमधिमुच्य पुनरेषां स्व-

---

[a] **Cee** GST 1.1

---

1 **sthitāṃ** G : **sthitā** A; **vyavasthitāṃ** B ◦ **tathā** G (de bzhin du T) : **tato** A; **tataḥ** B ◦ **tṛtīye** AB : **tṛtīye tu** G **2** **maitreyaṃ** AG : **maitreya°** B ◦ **vajrapāṇiṃ** AG : **vajrapāṇi°** B ◦ **khagarbbhaṃ** BG : **///kāśagarbhaṃ** A **3** paścima° BG; paścim{e}a° A ◦ **lokeśvaraṃ** A : **lokeśvara°** B; **lokeśaṃ** G ◦ **mañjughoṣaṃ** G ('jam pa'i dbyaṅs T) : **maṃjuśriyaṃ** A; **mañjuśriyaṃ** B **4** **dakṣiṇadvāre** A (lho'i sgor T) : **dakṣiṇe** BG **5** **paścimadvāre** AB (nub kyi sgor T) : **paścime** G ◦ **uttaradvāre** AB (byaṅ gi sgor T) : **uttare** G **7** **ūrddhvaṃm** A : **ūrddhe** B; **ūrddham** G ◦ uṣṇīṣa° AB : uṣṇī° G ◦ nisumbha° AB : niśumbha° G **9** **<ca>** em. (GST) : om. ABG; but cf. svacchaṃ tattsvabhāvam iti PU 19,9 ◦ **ca** AB (GST) : om. G **11** svacchādi° AB : svā¦cchādi° G

कायमण्डले स्कन्धस्वभावेन पञ्चबुद्धान्धातुस्वभावेन विद्यादेवता रूपादिविषयस्वभावेन रूपवज्रादिका आयतनस्वभावेन [B3] बोधिसत्त्वान- [A3G1] [G15b] वयवस्वभावेन क्रोधराजान्विन्यसेत् । अस्य सूत्रं सप्तदशपटले —

[b] पञ्च स्कन्धाः समासेन पञ्च बुद्धाः प्रकीर्तिताः । [B4]
वज्रायतनान्येव बोधिसत्त्वाग्रमण्डलम् ॥

पृथिवी लोचनाख्याता अब्धातुर्मामकी स्मृता ।
तेजश्च पाण्डराख्याता [G2] वायुस्तारा [B5] प्रकीर्तिता ॥ [b]

[c] रूपशब्दादिभिर्मन्त्री देवता भावयेत्सदा ॥ [c]

इति । इममर्थवशं ज्ञात्वाह भगवान् सर्व[A4]बुद्धसमायोगडाकिनीजाल[B6]-संवरमहायोगतन्त्रे —

---

[b] **Cee** GST 17.50–51abcd [c] **Cee** GST 7.14ab (not in chapter 17); cf. also mkhas pas gzugs sgra la sogs pa || lha ñid du ni rtag tu bsgom || SVT P260b4–5; CMP 351,1 and 362,3

---

[2] **rūpādiviṣayasvabhāvena rūpavajrādikāḥ | āyatanasvabhāvena bodhisattvān*** G : **āyatanasvabhāvena bodhisattvān* | ‹rūpaviṣyasvabhāvena caturdevyā›** B; **āyatanasvabhāvena bodhisattvān** A; rūpādiviṣayasvabhāvena rūpavajrādikāḥ n.e. T [3] **vinyaset⁰** B; **vinyaset*** G (rnam par dgod par bya'o T) : **vicintayet⁰** A ○ **saptadaśapaṭale** AG (le'u bcu bdun pa las T) : **saptamapaṭale** B [4] **samāsena** AB (mdor bsdus na T; GST) : **svabhāvena** G [5] **vajrāyatanāny eva** AB (GST; rdo rje skye mched ñid kyaṅ ni T) : **vajrāyatanair eva** G; kyaṅ add. T; pāda c unmetrical [7] **tejaś <ca>** em. (CMP 357,18) : **tejaḥ** ABG [8] **devatāṃ** BG (GST, CMP) : **devatā** A [9] **jñātvāha bhagavān*** B (mkhyen nas ... bcom ldan 'das kyis gsuṅs pa T) : **jñātvā bhagavān āha** G; **jñātvā bhagavān*** A

[d] अतत्त्वाशययोगानां देवतालम्बनं प्रति ।
प्रतिबिम्बमयो योगो निषिक्तादिषु जायते॥ [G3]

B6a सुतत्त्वाशययोगानां देवतालम्बनेन किम् । [B1]
आत्मयोगस्वसमयात्सिध्यते परमाक्षरम् ॥ [d]

[e] आत्मा वै सर्वबुद्धत्वं सर्वसौरित्वमेव च ।
तस्मात्सर्वप्रयत्नेन ह्यात्मानं पूजयेत्सदा ॥ [e] [B2G4]

इति ॥

TD199a1 TP171b7 [III.1.4] एवं बाह्यमण्डलं कायमण्डले ऽनुप्रवेश्य सर्वतथागतपरमाणु- [A5] परिघटितं स्वकायमण्डलमधिमुच्य पुनः कायमण्डलदेवतान्स्कन्ध- [B3] धात्वायतनस्वभावान् यथानुक्रमेण लीनान्परमार्थमण्डले प्रवेश्य तृ- [G5] तीयपटलोक्त-[f]ओं शून्यताज्ञानवज्रस्वभावात्मको ऽहमिति[f]मन्त्रेण ध- [B4] र्मकायं दृढीकुर्यात् । अस्य सूत्रं सप्तमपटले —

---

d **Cee** SBS P165a3–4 **e** **Cee** SBS P165a6; cf. PK 3.28, PU 19,1, CMP 366,3–4
f **Ce** GST 11,16

---

1 atatvāśaya° AG : atatvā{a}śaya° B **2** **jāyate** B (SBS) : **na jāyate** AG **4** **ātmayogasvasamayāt** em. (raṅ gi dam tshig bdag sbyor ba SBS) : **ātmayogaś ca samayāt** A; **ātmayogaṃ svasamayā**t* B; **ātmayoge svasamayāt*** G; sva n.e. T **5** °**sauritvam** A : °**śauritvam** BG; mchog T for sauri **6** °**prayatnena hy ātmānaṃ** A : °**prayatnenātmānaṃ** BG ○ pūjayet AG : pūjayet{i} B **8** **bāhyamaṇḍalaṃ kāyamaṇḍale** AG (phyi rol gyi dkyil 'khor lus kyi dkyil 'khor la T) : **bāhyamaṇḍale** B **9** °**parighaṭitaṃ** A : °**parighaṭita**° G; °**ghaṭitaṃ** B ○ °**maṇḍala**° G (dkyil 'khor gyi T) : °**maṇḍale** AB **10** **yathānukrameṇa** AB : **yathākrameṇa** G **11** **tṛtīyapaṭalokta oṃ** A (le'u gsum pa las gsuṅs pa'i | oṃ T) : **tṛtīyapaṭaloktaṃ | oṃ** B; **tṛtīyapaṭale py ukta | oṃ** G ○ °**mantreṇa** AB : **anena mantreṇa** G (anena n.e. T)

[g]समयात्क्षरेद्देतं विधिना पिबेत्फलकाङ्क्षया।
मारयेत्ताथागतं व्यूहं सुतरां सिद्धिमाप्नुयात् ॥[g]

[III.1.5] [h]एवं शून्यतालम्बनेन सकलक्लेशमलं प्रक्षाल्य तस्मादात्मानं वज्रसत्त्वमहामुद्रारूपं निष्पादयेदनेन क्रमेण। तत्रायं क्रमः — परमार्थसत्यात्सूर्यमण्डलम्' तदुपरि चन्द्रमण्डलं' पुनस्तदुपरि रक्ताष्टदलपद्मं' पद्मोपरि ओं आः हूं इत्यक्षरत्रयमुपर्युपरि विन्यस्य सर्वं संहृत्य परिपूर्णचन्द्रमण्डलाकारपरिणतं चित्तमात्रं ध्यात्वा तस्मिञ्जगत्स्थावरजङ्गममन्तर्भाव्य तृतीयपटलोक्त-[i]ओं धर्मधातुस्वभावात्मको ऽहमि[i]तिमन्त्रेण स्वचित्तरत्नं दृढीकुर्यात् । इत्ययं प्रथमो योगः ॥[h] TD199a3 TP172a3 B6b A3b

इममर्थं द्योतयन्नाह संवरे — TD199a6 TP172a6

[j]ज्ञानमात्रसमापत्तिर्योग इत्यभिधीयते ॥[j]

इति ॥

[III.2] [k]ततश्चन्द्रमण्डलोपरि त्र्यक्षरम्' तस्माद्वज्रम्' वज्रान्महावज्रधर- TD199a7 TP172a6

---

[g] Ce GST 7.33 [h] Ci'e VNU* 12b5–13a4 [i] Cee GST 12,18 [j] Ce SBS P200b3
[k] Cf. VNU* 13a5–b2

---

[1] vidhinā BG : vidhinām' A ∘ pāda ab unmetrical [3] prakṣālya AG : prakhyā'lya B [4] **tatrāyaṃ kramaḥ** G : om. AB (tatrāyaṃ kramaḥ n.e. T) [5] **candra°** AB : **pūrṇṇacandra°** G (pūrṇa n.e. T) [7] **vinyasya** AG (VNU*) : **nyasya** B [8] **jagat** AG ('gro ba T; VNU*) : om. B ∘ **tṛtīyapaṭalokta oṃ** A : **tṛtīyapaṭalokta | oṃ** B; **tṛtīyapaṭaloktaṃ | oṃ** G [10] **ayaṃ prathamo yogaḥ** em. ('di ni daṅ po'i rnal 'byor ro T) : **ayaṃ prathamayogaḥ** A; **ayaṃ prathamopayogaḥ** B; **prathamo yogaḥ** G [13] **iti** AG : om. B

रूपमात्मानं शुक्लवर्णं ध्यायात् ।

[l] वज्रसत्त्वो महाराजा वैरोचनसमप्रभः ॥ [l]

इति पञ्चदशपटले वचनात् । द्वितीयो ऽनुयोगः ॥ [k]

TD199b1 TP172a8 G16a अस्य सूत्रमेकादशपटले—

[m] त्रिवज्राक्षरमन्त्राग्रैर्महामुद्राविभावनम् ।
कर्तव्यं ज्ञानवज्रेण सर्वबोधिसमावहम् ॥ [m]

इति ॥

TD199b2 TD172b1 [III.3.1] [n] एवं योगानुयोगक्रमेणात्मानं सम्भोगकायं सम्पाद्य चरमभविकवत्सत्त्वार्थं प्रति स्कन्धधात्वायतनानुप्रवेशेन निर्माणकायमात्मानं निष्पादयेदनेन क्रमेण। तत्रायं क्रमः — ओंकारं शुक्लवर्णं B7a वैरोचनात्मकं मस्तके विन्यस्य रूपस्कन्धं प्रवेशयेत् । एवमाःकारं रक्तवर्णममिताभात्मकं मुखे विन्यस्य सञ्ज्ञास्कन्धं प्रवेशयेत् । हूंकारं कृष्णवर्णमक्षोभ्यात्मकं हृदये विन्यस्य विज्ञानस्कन्धं प्रवे-

[l] **Cee** GST 15.35cb [m] **Ce** GST 11.1 [n] **Ci'e** VNU* 13b2–4

1 ātmānaṃ BG : ātmana'ṃ A **2** vajra° AG : vajr{e}a° B **4** **ekādaśapaṭale** em. (le'u bcu gcig pa las T) : **daśamapaṭale** ABG **9** **caramabhavika**° BG (VNU*) : **caramabhavika‹bodhisatva›**° A (bodhisattva n.e. T) ○ **satvā**° AG (VNU*) : **sarvvasatvā**° B (sarva n.e. T) ○ srid pa tha mal pa'i sems can gyi don gyi phyir T for caramabhavikavat sattvārthaṃ prati **12** **raktavarṇṇam** AG : **raktaṃ** B **13** **kṛṣṇavarṇṇam** G; **kṛṣṇavarṇṇaṃ** B : **kṛṣṇam** A ○ akṣobhya° AG : a{'}kṣobhya° B

शयेत्* । स्वाकारं पीतवर्णं रत्नसम्भवात्मकं नाभौ विन्यस्य वेदना-
स्कन्धं प्रवेशयेत् । हाकारं हरि*तवर्णममोघसिद्ध्यात्मकं B3 पादयोर्विन्यस्य
संस्कारस्कन्धं G4 प्रवेशयेत् ॥n

[III.3.2] मोहरती*ति लोचनां पृथिवीधातुस्वभावेन। द्वेषरती*ति मामकी- Td199b5 Tp172b4
मब्धातुस्वभावेन। B4 रागरती*ति पाण्डरां तेजोधातुस्वभावेन। A5 वज्ररती*ति
तारां* वायुधातुस्वभावेन विन्यस्य G5 खरत्वं द्रवतामौष्ण्यं* प्रेरणत्वं B5 प्रक-
ल्पयेत् ॥

[III.3.3] थ्लीं* क्षितिगर्भं* चक्षुरायतनस्वभावेन। ओं वज्रपाणिं श्रोत्रा- Td199b6 Tp172b6
यतनस्वरूपेण*। ओं आकाशगर्भं घ्राणायतनरूपेण*। ओं लोकेश्वरं* B6
जिह्वायतनस्वरूपेण*। G6 हूं मञ्जुश्रियं मनआयतनस्वरूपेण*। ओं सर्व-
निवरणविष्कम्भिणं A6 कायायतनस्वरूपेण विन्यस्य दिव्यलोचनादीन्प्र*- B1 B7b
कल्पयेत् । मैंबीजं मैत्रेयं स्नायु*स्वभावेन न्यसेत् । संबीजं समन्तभद्रं G7
सर्वशरीरसन्धिस्वभावे*न न्यसे*दिति ॥

[III.3.4] एवं मन्त्राधि*ष्ठाने स्कन्धधात्वायतनमापूर्य B2 दीर्घहूंकारा*न्दश- Td200a2 Tp173a1

---

1 praveśayet* B; praveśayet* G : praveśaśa'yet* A **2** **harita°** BG (ljaṅ gu T) : **arakta°** A **4** **moharatīti** BG : **moharatir iti** A ○ **dveṣaratīti** BG : **dveṣaratir iti** A **5** **rāgaratīti** BG : **rāgaratir iti** A ○ **vajraratīti** BG : **vajraratir iti** A **6** tārāṃ G; tārām B : ‹tārāṃ› A ○ **dravatāṃ auṣṇyaṃ** G : **dravatāṃ causṇyaṃ** AB **8** **thlīṃ** A; **{thlīṃ} ‹thlīṃ›** B : **thlīṃkāraṃ** G; oṃ T for thlīṃ ○ **kṣitigarbbhaṃ** B : **kṣigarbbhaṃ** G; **kṣitigarbhabījaṃ** A **9** **°svarūpeṇa** AG : **°svabhāvena** B ○ **°rūpeṇa** AG : **°svabhāvena** B ○ **lokeśvaraṃ** G : **lokeśaṃ** AB **10** **jihvāyatanasvarūpeṇa** G; **jihvāyatanasva{bhāve}rūpeṇa** B : **jihvāy{ā}atanarūpeṇa** A ○ **°svarūpeṇa** G : **°rūpeṇa** A; **°svabhāvena** B **11** **divyalocanādīṃ** B (lha'i mig la sogs pa T) : **divyacakṣurādīṃ*** A; **locanādīṃ*** G **12** snāyu° BG : snāyuḥ A **13** **°svabhāvena** AB : **°bhāvena** G ○ **nyased** AB : **vinyased** G **14** **°ādhiṣṭhāne** AG : **°ādhiṣṭhānena** B ○ **°hūṃkārān*** A (hūṃ riṅ por T) : **°hūṃkārāt*** B; **°hūṃkārād** G

क्रोधान्भुजाद्यवयवे विन्यसेदनेन क्रमेण — तत्र दक्षिणभुजे यमा-
A4a न्तकम्' वामभुजे ऽपराजितम्' मुखे हयग्रीवम्' गुह्ये ऽमृ-
तकुण्डलिम्' दक्षिणबाहावचलम्' वामबाहौ टक्किराजम्' द-
क्षिणजानौ नीलदण्डम्' वामजानौ महाबलम्' मूर्ध्न्युष्णीषचक्र-
वर्तिनम्' पादयोर्निसुम्भराजं विन्यस्य दशदिशो ऽनुप्रवेशयेदिति।
अस्य सूत्रं <u>प्रथमपटले</u> — °महाविद्यापुरुषमूर्तिं सर्वतथागत-
मन्त्राधिष्ठानमधिष्ठापयामास। समनन्तराधिष्ठितमात्रे स एव भगवान्बो-
G16b धिचित्तवज्रस्तथागतस्त्रिमुखाकारेण सर्वतथागतैः सन्दृश्यते स्मेति°।
तृतीयो ऽतियोगः ॥

Tᴅ200a5 Tᴘ173a6 [III.4.1] ᵖएवं साधको योगत्रयेणात्मनः प्राकृताहङ्कारमपनीय श्रीवज्र-
B8a सत्त्वरूपं निष्पाद्य पुनर्घटमाननिष्पन्नदेवताविकल्पापनयनार्थं चतुर्थं
महायोगं कुर्यात्।ᵖ तत्र ओंकारं शुक्लवर्णं मस्तके ध्यात्वा त-
ज्जनितलोचनाव्यूहमाधिपत्यप्रयोगेण गगनकुहरे विचिन्तयेत्।
ततो झटिति वैरोचनव्यूहमाधिपत्यप्रयोगेणान्तरीक्षे दृष्ट्वा <u>द्वादशपट-</u>

ᵒ **Cee** GST 5,23–6,1 ᵖ **Ci'e** VNU* 15a1–2

---

2 **vāma**° AG : **vāyu**° B 3 'mṛtakuṇḍalim AG : 'mṛtaku{ma}ṇḍalim B ○ **vāmabāhau** AB : **vāme** G 4 **dakṣiṇa**° AB : **dakṣiṇe** G 5 pādayor BG : pādayo! A ○ nisumbha° AB : niśumbha° G ○ **iti** AG : om. B 6 °**mūrtiṃ** em. (GST; PU 20.28) : °**mūrtiḥ** ABG 7 °**tathāgatamantrādhiṣṭhānam** A (de bźin gśegs pa thams cad kyi sṅags kyis byin gyis brlabs T) : °**tathāgatādhiṣṭhānam** BG ○ **bhagavān*** G (GST) : om. AB; bhagavat n.e. T 9 tṛtīyo BG : tīyo! A 10 **yogatrayeṇātmanaḥ** G : **yogatritayenātmanaḥ** A; **yogatrayam ātmanaḥ** B; rnal 'byor gsum gyi bdag ñid kyis T 11 yaṅ add. T ○ punar BG : puna! A ○ **ghaṭamānaniṣpannadevatā**° G (VNU*) : **ghaṭamāno niṣpannadevatā**° A; **ghaṭamāno niṣpannadevatā** | B; bya ba ni yoṅs su rdzogs pa'i lha'i T 13 °vyūham ādhipatya° AB : °vyūham aha!dhipatya° G ○ dbyiṅs T for kuhara 14 bsams nas T for dṛṣṭvā

लोक्तगाथाद्वयेनाध्येषयेत् । तत्रेयं गाथा —

[q][r]बुद्धकाय[G3]धरः श्री[B3]मांस्त्रिवज्राभेद्यभावितः ।
अधिष्ठानपदं मे ऽद्य करोतु कायवज्रिणः ॥

दशदिक्संस्थिता बुद्धास्त्रिवज्राभे[A4]द्यभाविताः ।
अधिष्ठानपदं मे ऽद्य कु[B4]र्वन्तु कायवज्रिणः ॥[q]

अध्येषणानन्तरं देवताव्यूहमन्योन्यानुरागणपूर्वकं परमानन्दसुखमनुभूय श्वेतरश्मिस्वभावेन ज्ञानसत्त्व[G4]व[B5]द्वैरोचनद्वारेण प्रविश्य ज्ञानभूमिं प्राप्य समस्तकायमापूर्य प्रीणयन्तं विचिन्त्य सप्तमपटलोक्तगाथया दृढीकुर्यात् । तत्रेयं गाथा —

[s]यत्कायं [B6]सर्वबुद्धानां पञ्च[A5]स्कन्धप्रपूरितम् ।
बुद्धकाय[G5]स्वभावेन ममापि तादृशं भवेत् ॥[s]

इति। ततः षष्ठपटलोक्तमन्त्रेणाद्वयाहङ्कारं कुर्यात् — [t]ओं [B1] सर्वतथा- B8b
गतकायवज्रस्वभावात्मको ऽह[r][t]मिति ॥

---

[q] **Cee** GST 12.70–71 [r] **Ci'e** VNU* 15a5–b5 [s] **Ce** GST 7.28 [t] **Ce** GST 17,7

---

1 le'u gñis pa T for dvādaśapaṭala **6** anyonyānurāg{e}aṇa° G : anyonya'n{ā}urāgaṇa° A; anyonyāa'nurāgaṇa° B **7** anubhūya BG : anur'bhūya A ○ ye śes sems dpa'i raṅ bźin du T for jñānasattvavat **8** **samasta**° G (VNU*) : **samastaṃ** AB ○ **saptama**° G; **sapta‹ma›**° B : **sapta**° A ○ °**gāth{ā}ayā** B : °**gāthāyā** A; °**gāthā** G **9** tatra n.e. T **12** **iti** B : om. AG; iti n.e. T ○ **ṣaṣṭhapaṭalo**° em. (le'u drug pa las T) : **saptamapaṭalo**° ABG

TD200b4 TP173b5 [III.4.2] [u]वाक्चित्तयोरप्यनेनैव क्रमेणाधिष्ठानं कुर्यात् । तत्रायं क्रमः — आःकारं रक्तवर्णं मुखपद्मोपरि विन्यस्य तज्जनितपाण्डरवासिनीव्यूहैर्गगनमापूर्य पूर्ववदमिताभव्यूहं दृष्ट्वाध्येषयेदनया गाथया —

[v]धर्मो वै वाक्पथः श्रीमांस्त्रिवज्राभेद्यभावितः ।
अधिष्ठानपदं मे ऽद्य करोतु वाग्वज्रिणः ॥

दशदिक्संस्थिता बुद्धास्त्रिवज्राभेद्यभाविताः ।
अधिष्ठानपदं मे ऽद्य कुर्वन्तु वाग्वज्रिणः ॥[v]

एवमध्येषिते पूर्ववद्द्वयेन्द्रियसमापत्त्या महारागानलेन व्यूहद्वयं द्रवीभूय रक्तरश्मिरूपेण मुखे प्रविश्याशेषवागैश्वर्यमापादयन्तं विचिन्त्य दृढीकुर्यादनया गाथया — (A4b)

[w]यदेव वज्रधर्मस्य वाचा निरुक्तिसम्पदः ।
ममापि तादृशी वाचा भवेद्धर्मधरोपमा ॥[w]

---

[u] **Ci'e** VNU* 15b5–16a5 [v] **Cee** GST 12.72–73 [w] **Cee** GST 7.29

---

1 sku daṅ gsuṅ daṅ thugs kyi T for vākcittayoḥ ◦ api n.e. T ◦ **anenaiva** B; **{ā}anenaiva** A : **anena** G; eva n.e. T **2** āḥkāraṃ BG; ā⟨ḥ⟩kāraṃ A ◦ mgrin pa'i padma'i T for mukhapadma ◦ **vinyasya** AB (bkod nas T) : **vinyaset*** G ◦ °pāṇḍara° AB; °pāṇḍara{¨}° G **3** °vyūhair BG : °vyūhai! A ◦ **gaganam** AB : **gaganatalam** G (tala n.e. T) **5** pāda d unmetrical ◦ vāgvajriṇaḥ AG : vāgva{ve}jriṇaḥ B **7** pāda d unmetrical ◦ vāgvajriṇaḥ AG : vā|g^{0}vajriṇaḥ B **8** **mahārāgānalena** AB ('dod chags chen po'i mes T) : **mahārāganaya**° G **9** **mukhe** BG : **mukhye** A ◦ āpādayantaṃ G; āpādayaṃtaṃ B : āpādayanta! A **10** gāthayā G; {th}gāth{ā}ayā A; gāth{ā}ayā B **12** °**opamā** B : °**opamām** A; °**opamaḥ** G

इति। ततो ऽनेन मन्त्रेणाद्वैधीकाराहङ्कारं कुर्यात् । तत्रायं मन्त्रः —
[x] ओं सर्वतथागतवाग्वज्रस्वभावात्मको ऽहमिति ॥ [x] B9a

[III.4.3] [y] ततः स्वहृदि वज्रवरटके कृष्णवर्णं हूंकारं विचिन्त्य तज्जनित- Tᴅ201a2 Tᴘ174a3
मामकीव्यूहं गगनकुहरे विचिन्त्य पूर्ववज्झटित्यक्षोभ्यव्यूहं चान्तरीक्षे G17a
दृष्ट्वा प्रार्थयेदनया गाथया —

[z] वज्रचित्तधरः श्रीमांस्त्रिवज्राभेद्यभावितः ।
अधिष्ठानपदं मे ऽद्य करोतु चित्तवज्रिणः ॥

दशदिक्संस्थिता बुद्धास्त्रिवज्राभेद्यभाविताः ।
अधिष्ठानपदं मे ऽद्य कुर्वन्तु चित्तवज्रिणः ॥ [z]

प्रार्थनानन्तरं पूर्ववद्व्यूहद्वयं महारागानलेन द्रवीभूय कृष्णरश्मिरूपेण हृदये प्रविश्य चित्तैश्वर्यं सम्पादयन्तं विचिन्त्य दृढीकुर्यादनया गाथया —

[a] यच्चित्तं समन्तभद्रस्य गुह्यकेन्द्रस्य धीमतः ।
ममापि तादृशं चित्तं भवेद्वज्रधरोपमम् ॥ [a]

---

[x] **Ce** GST 17,10 [y] **Ci'e** VNU* 16b1–6 [z] **Cee** GST 12.74–75 [a] **Ce** GST 7.30

---

1 **iti** AB (ces gsuṅs so T) : om. G ○ tatas n.e. T **3** yaṅ add. T ○ **svahṛdi** AB : **svahṛdi candramaṇḍalopari** G (candramaṇḍalopari n.e. T) **4** kuhara n.e. T ○ **cāntarīkṣe** B (VNU*) : **āntarīkṣe** G; **¨ntarīkṣe** A; ca n.e. T **5** anayā gāthayā BG : anaṃ[!] gāth{ā}ayā A **10** gñis su med pa'i 'dod chags chen po'i mes T for vyūhadvayaṃ mahārāgānalena **13** pāda a hypermetric ○ **guhyakendrasya** AB : **guhyendrasya** G **14** thugs T for vajra

इति। ततो ऽनेनाद्वैधीकाराहङ्कारं कुर्यात् — ओं सर्वतथागतचित्तवज्रस्वभावात्मको ऽहमिति ॥

TD201a6 TP174a8 [III.4.4] एवं कुलत्रयप्रवेशेन कायवाक्चित्तं पृथगधिष्ठाय पुनस्त्रिवज्राभेद्यस्वभावेन महावज्रधराधिष्ठानं कुर्यादनेन क्रमेण — ओं सर्वतथागतकायवाक्चित्तवज्रस्वभावात्मको ऽहमिति। B9b अस्य सूत्रं द्वितीयपटले — उत्पादयन्तु भवन्तश्चित्तं कायाकारेण कायं चित्ताकारेण चित्तं वाक्प्रव्याहारेणेति। प्रथमपटलोक्तसमयोद्भववज्रसमाधिन्यायेन निष्पन्नत्वात्समयसत्त्व इत्युच्यते ॥

TD201b1 TP174b3 [III.4.5] एवं त्रिमुखं षड्भुजं समयसत्त्वं निष्पाद्य तस्य हृदये ज्ञानसत्त्वं द्विभुजं रक्तवर्णं सम्पुटयोगेन सर्वशरीरं प्रीणयन्तं विचिन्त्य स्वमुकुटे ऽधिपतिं ध्यायात्। अस्य सूत्रं द्वादशपटले —

सर्वाकारवरोपेतं स्वकायवाक्चित्तवज्रिणम्।
हृदये ज्ञानसमयं मुकुटे वज्राग्रधारिणम् ॥

[b] **Ce** GST 17,4 [c] **Ci'e** VNU* 16b6–17a1 [d] **Ce** GST 17,24 [e] **Ce** GST 9,13–14 [f] **Ci'e** VNU* 17a2–4 [g] **Cee** GST 12.45–46

1 °**opamam iti** G : °**opamam*** A; °**opamaḥ** B ○ gñis su med pa'i rnam pa'i T for advaidhīkāra ○ °**āhaṃkāraṃ kuryāt*** G (ṅa rgyal bya ste T) : °**ālambanaṃ kuryā**t* B; °**ālambanaṃ** A **3** kulatraya° G; kula{pu}traya° B : kulapu'traya° A ○ pṛthag adhi° G; pṛthag{ā}adhi° B : pṛthag* dhi!° A **4** °**svabhāvena** BG (raṅ bźin gyis T) : °**bhāvena** A ○ kramena n.e. T **9** **hṛdaye** AB (sñiṅ gar T) : **hṛdayena** G **10** **sarva**° BG (VNU*) : **sarvaṃ** A ○ °mukuṭe AG : °makuṭe B **12** pāda b hypermetrical (cf. kāyavākcittavajriṇaṃ GST) **13** mukuṭe AG : makuṭe B

प्रीणनं सर्वबुद्धानामिदं समयमुत्तमम् ।
कर्तव्यं समयाग्रेण सर्वसिद्धिकरं परम् ॥[g]

[h]एवं समयसत्त्वहृदये ज्ञानसत्त्वं विचिन्त्य ज्ञानसत्त्वस्यापि हृदये हूंकारं समाधिसत्त्वाख्यं सततोदयं बृहत्प्रदीपसदृशमज्ञानान्धकारविधमनार्थमालोकपुञ्जाकारं ध्यायादिति ।[h] अस्य सूत्रमेकादशपटले —

[i]बुद्धमण्डलमध्यस्थं वज्राक्षोभ्यं प्रभावयेत् ।
हूंकारं हृदये ध्यात्वा चित्तं बिन्दुगतं न्यसेत् ॥[i] A5a

इति । महायोगः ॥

[IV.1] [j]एवं योगचतुष्टयेनात्मानं त्रिसत्त्वात्मकं स्वार्थसम्पत्स्वभावं स- TD201b5 TP174b8
माधिराजाग्रीं निष्पाद्येदानीं परार्थसम्पत्तये मण्डलराजाग्रीसमाधिप्र- B10a
दर्शनाय पीठिकावतार्यते । भगवाञ्छाक्यमुनिः सर्वं कृत्वा तुषितव-
रभुवनादवतीर्य वीतरागरूपमभिनिर्माय श्रावकगोत्राञ्छ्रावकमार्गे G17b
प्रतिष्ठाप्य पुनर्महायानिकबोधिसत्त्वानां पारमितामार्गं प्रकाश्य

---

[h] **Ci'e** VNU* 17a4–5 [i] **Ce** GST 11.42 [j] **Ci'e** VNU* 17b1–18b3

---

1 sarva n.e. T ◦ samayam uttamaṃ AB : samayamu'uttamaṃ G 2 dam tshig kun T for samayāgra ◦ param n.e. T 3 **prīṇanaṃ ... jñānasatvaṃ** AG : om. B ◦ **jñānasattvasyāpi** AG (ye śes sems dpa'i T) : **jñānasyāpi** B; api n.e. T 9 °**sampat***° B; °**saṃpat***° A (VNU*) : °**saṃpatti**° G 12 thams cad mkhyen pa mdzad nas add. T ◦ °**mārge** A; °**mār{¨}ge** B (VNU*) : °**mārggeṇa** G; sa la T for mārge 13 sems can T for bodhisattva ◦ pha rol tu phyin pa'i tshul thams cad T for pāramitāmārga

गम्भीराधिमुक्तिकानां रागजबोधिप्रदर्शनार्थमेतत् । तत्र प्रथमपटलोक्तमहारागनयं नाम [B3] समाधिं समापन्नस्तथा घटमानयोगिनाप्यादियोगं कृत्वा रागचरितसत्त्वानां काममोक्षप्रदर्शनाय सप्तदशपट[A3]लोक्तसर्वकामोपभोगसमाधिना [B4] विहर्तव्यमनेन क्रमेण। तत्रायं क्रमः — [G2] [B5] सर्वलक्षणोपेतां बाह्याङ्गनां मन्त्रतन्त्रसुशिक्षितामादाय पुरतो ऽवस्थाप्य पञ्चकुलकलापिनीं कुर्यात् । ततो वज्रपद्मसंस्कारपूर्वकं द्वयेन्द्रियसमापत्तिं कृत्वा [B6] बोधिचित्तादक्षोभ्यादिमण्डलचक्रमभिनिर्माय तत्तत्समाधिना [G3] सत्त्वानां [A4] द्वेषादिक्लेशान्विशोध्य पुनरानीय स्वकायम-
B10b ण्डले प्रवेशयेत् । [B1] अथ वा स्वहृदयाज्ज्ञानमुद्रामभिनिर्माय तया सह समापत्तिं कृत्वा मन्त्रैकनिर्माणात्सत्त्वार्थं कुर्यात् ।

[k] हृदयस्था [G4] महादेवी योगिनां [B2] योगवाहिनी ।

---

[k] **Cee** SRT 45; also cited in PU 48,12–13, YM 14a4

---

[1] °**bodhipradarśanārtham** G (VNU*) : °**bodhipadapradarśanārtham** A; °**bodhipraṇayanārthaṃ** B; byaṅ chub ’di bstan pa’i don du T for °bodhipradarśanārtham etat ○ **etat*** || **tatra** A : **etattantra**° B; **etat*tantre** G (tantra n.e. T) [2] °paṭalokta° AB : °paṭalokta{prathamapa}° G ○ de la add. T [4] prathamapaṭalokta° ... °saptadaśapaṭalokta° n.e. Tp ○ **mahārāganayaṃ ... saptadaśapaṭalokta|**° B; **mahārāganayan ... saptadaśapaṭalokta**° A : **‹mahārāganayaṃ ... saptadaśapaṭaloktaḥ›** G ○ tiṅ ṅge ’dzin ’di yis T for °samādhinā ○ le’u bcu bdun pa las gsuṅs pa’i rim pa ’dis T for saptadaśapaṭalokta° ... anena kramena [5] **bāhyāṅganāṃ** AB : **bāhyāṅganā** G; phyag rgya T for aṅganā ○ purato AB : pu¨to G [6] brtag par bya’o T for °kalāpinīṃ kuryāt [7] **bodhicittād akṣoḅhyādi**° AG : **bodhicittākṣobhyādi**° B [8] **tattat**° AB (de daṅ de T; VNU*) : **tat**° G ○ °**kleśān** A (VNU*) : °**kleśagaṇān** BG (gaṇa n.e. T) [9] **svahṛdayā**t* B (VNU*) : **svahṛdaya**° A; **svahṛdaye** G; sñiṅ gar T for svahṛdayāt [10] **samāpattiṃ** BG (sñoms par bźugs par T) : **sampattiṃ** A ○ °nirmāṇāt A; °nirmmāṇā t* B : °nirmāṇād {vā} G

जननी सर्वबुद्धानां वज्रधात्वीश्वरी स्मृता ॥[k]

इति सर्वरहस्यतन्त्रे[j] वचनात् । अस्य सूत्रं सप्तमपटले—

[l] तां षोडशाब्दिकां [A5] प्राप्य योषितं कान्तिसुप्रभाम् [B3] ।
प्रच्छन्ने प्रारभेत्पूजामधिष्ठानपदैस्त्रिभिः [G5] ॥
ताथागतीं महाभार्यां लोचनां वा विभावयेत् ।
द्वयेन्द्रियसमापत्त्या बुद्धसिद्धिमवाप्नुयात् [B4] ॥[l]

इति ॥

[IV.2] [m] एवं बाह्याध्यात्मिकमुद्रां निश्चित्येदानीं पञ्चकुलकलापिनीक्रमः प्रदर्श्यते । ओंकारं [G6] शिरस्याःकारं मुखे हूं हृदये स्वा नाभौ [B5] हा पाद[A6]योर्न्यसेत् । चतुर्धातुस्वभावेन लोचनादीन्न्यसेत् । रूपादिविषयस्वभावेन रूपवज्रादीन्न्यसेत् । पुनस्तस्या भुजाद्यवयवेषु [B6] क्रोधराज्ञी[G7]र्न्यसेत् । [m] तत्र दक्षिणभुजे वज्रवेतालीं वामभुजे ऽपराजितां मुखे भृ- TD202a7 TP175b1

---

[l] **Cee** GST 7.17–18 [m] **Ci'e** VNU* 18b3–19a1

---

1 sarva n.e. T ○ vajradhātvīśvarī BG; vajradhātvī{śva}śvarī A **3** **<tāṃ>** em. : om. ABG (n.e. T; but cf. tāṃ tāṃ GST; tām iti PU 67,14) ○ **yoṣitaṃ** G (PU 66,24) : **yoṣitāṃ** AB ○ śin tu yid 'oṅ ma T for kāntisuprabhā **5** **vā vibhāvayet*** A; **vā vibhāvaye**t* B (GST; PU 67,4) : **pravibhāvayet*** G **6** °samāpattyā A : °samāpatyā! BG **8** **bāhyādhyātmika**° AG (phyi naṅ gi T) : **bāhyātmika**° B ○ brtag pa'i T for kalāpinī **9** **āḥkāraṃ** BG : **āḥ** A **10** **pādayor** B; **p///dayor** A : **dvipādayor** G ○ °**ādīr** em. : °**ādīn*** A; **ādīn** B; **ādīn⁰** G ○ **rūpādiviṣaya**° G (VNU*); **cakṣurādyāyatana**° AB; mig la sogs pa'i skye mched T **11** °**ādīr** em. : °**ādīn*** A; **ādīn** BG ○ cakṣurādyātanasvabhāvena bodhisatvān nyaset* add. G (n.e. T) ○ **bhujādy**° BG : ‹**hastā**›**dy**° A ○ °**avayaveṣu** B (yan lag rnams la T) : °**avayave** AG **12** °**rājñīr** B : °**rājñīṃ** AG ○ de'i T for tatra ○ °vetālīṃ G : °vettā!līṃ AB

B11a कुटीं गुह्य एकजटां पुनर्दक्षिणबाहौ विश्ववज्रीं वामबाहौ [B1] विश्वरत्नीं द-
A5b क्षिणजानौ विश्वपद्मीं वामजानौ [A1] विश्वकर्मीं मूर्ध्नि [G8] गगनवज्रिणीं पादयो-
र्धरणीन्धरीं न्यसेदिति । अस्य सूत्रमष्टमपटले—

स्तनान्तरं यावच्छिखान्तमध्ये
[B2] चरणान्तरे चापि न्यसेद्विधिज्ञः ।
नाभीकटीगुह्य जिनात्मजानां
न्यासं प्रकुर्यात्कुलपञ्चकानाम् ॥

इति ॥

Tᴅ202b5 Tᴘ175b7 [IV.3] एवमभिसंस्कृत्य प्राकृत[B3]स्त्रीभाव[G9]मपनीय वज्रपद्मसंस्कारं कुर्यादनेन
क्रमेण । हूंकारेण [A2] स्वलिङ्गं पञ्चसूचिकं वज्रं विचिन्त्य मध्यसूचौ प्रणवं
न्यसेदिति वज्रसंस्कारः [B4]। आःकारं तस्या धर्मोदये विन्यस्य तज्जनित-
G18a रक्ताष्टदलपद्मं ध्यायादिति पद्मसंस्कारः [G1]। अस्य सूत्रं सप्तमपटले —

हूंकारं च ओंकारं च फट्कारं च विकल्पयेत् ।
[B5] पञ्चरश्मिसमाकीर्णं वज्रं पद्मं च भावयेत् ॥

---

[n] **Cee** GST 8.9 [o] **Cee** GST 7.19

---

[1] cha T for bāhu ○ cha T for bāhu [2] °**padmīṃ** AB : °**padminīṃ** G [6] °**guhya** BG; °**guhya{ṃ}** A (cf. °guhya ity atra saptamīlopaḥ PU 75,26–27) [8] **iti** G; **{¨}i{¨}ti{ṃ}** A : om. B [9] °**bhāvam** AB : °**svabhāvam** G (raṅ bźin T) ○ byin gyis brlab par T for °saṃskāraṃ [10] °**sūcikaṃ** BG : °**sūci‹ka›**° A [11] **iti** G : om. AB ○ °saṃskāraḥ BG : °saṃskāra! A ○ **āḥkāraṃ** BG : om. A [12] **iti** G : om. AB [13] **oṃkārañ ca** BG : om. A [14] **ca** BG : om. A

इति ॥

[IV.4] [p] ततो रत्नसम्भवाहङ्कारवानन्योन्यानुरागणपूर्वकमालिङ्गनचुम्बना- TD202b7 TP176a1 दिकं कृत्वा षष्ठपटलोक्तमन्त्रेणाद्वयाहङ्कारं कुर्यात् । तत्रायं मन्त्रः — [q] ओं सर्वतथागतानुरागणवज्रस्वभावात्मको ऽहमिति रत्नसम्भ- B11b वाधिष्ठानम् । ततो हूंकारगीतमुदाहरन् योषित्कर्मस्थो भवेत् । क्षरणावस्थायां फट्कारमन्त्रमुच्चारयेत् । ततः कायमाण्डलेयदेवताः परमानन्दसुखमनुभूय नाडीविवराद्बिन्दुरूपेण पद्ममध्ये निपतन्ति । अस्य सूत्रं प्रथमपटले — [r] सर्वतथागतकायवाक्चित्तहृदयवज्रयोषिद्भगेषु विजहारेति । एवं बोधिचित्तावस्थायाममोघसिद्ध्यधिष्ठानमधिमुच्य षष्ठपटलोक्तपूजामन्त्रेणाद्वयाहङ्कारं कुर्यात् । तत्रायं मन्त्रः— [s] ओं सर्वतथागतपूजावज्रस्वभावात्मको ऽहमिति ॥[p]

[IV.5] [t] एवं पञ्चतथागतानुप्रवेशेनात्मानमधिष्ठाय समाध्यभिषेकपूजा- TD203a4 TP176a6 पर्यन्तं सर्वकुलात्मकाहङ्कारं कृत्वा परार्थसम्पत्तये भवोत्पत्तिक्रमेण

---

[p] **Ci'e** VNU* 19b1–5 [q] **Ce** GST 17,15 [r] **Ce** GST 4,4–5 [s] **Ce** GST 17,18 [t] **Ci'e** VNU* 19b5–20a1

---

2 de la T for tatas ○ °**pūrvakam** G; °**pūrvvakam** B : °**pūrvam** A **3** **ṣaṣṭhapaṭalo**° BG : **ṣaṭ*paṭalo**° A **4** °**ānurāgaṇa**° BG : °**ānurāga**° A ○ vajra n.e. T **5** °**ādhiṣṭhānaṃ** AB : °**āhaṃkāras** G; ṅa rgyal gyis bya'o T ○ **yoṣitkarmma**° B; **yoṣit*karma**° G : **karmma**° A; yoṣit n.e. T **6** **kāya**° BG (lus kyi T) : **kāyān** A **8** °**hṛdayavajra**° AG : om. B; hṛdaya n.e. T **10** rim pas T for mantreṇa **11** **iti** BG : om. A **12** evam n.e. T ○ **pañca‹ta›thāgatā**° B; **paṃcatathāgatā**° G : **pañcamatathāgatā**° A ○ °**abhiṣeka**° em. (VNU*) : °**abhiṣekaṃ** ABG **13** **sarvvakulātmakāhaṃkāraṃ** B; **sarvakulātmak{o}āhaṅkāraṃ** A (rigs thams cad kyi bdag ñid kyi ṅa rgyal T) : **sarvak{ā}rmmasārataraṃ** G ○ **bhavotpatti**° BG (srid pa skye ba'i T) : **tatvotpatti**° A

मण्डलचक्रमुत्सृजेत् ।[t] तत्राक्षोभ्यसमाधिना सत्त्वानां द्वेषक्लेशविशुद्धिं करोति। एवं वैरोचनसमाधिना मोहविशुद्धिम् । रत्नसम्भवसमाधिना मानविशुद्धिम् । अमिताभसमाधिना रागविशु-
B12a द्धिम् । अमोघसिद्धिसमाधिनेर्ष्याविशुद्धिम् । स एव भगवान्लोचनासमाधिना सत्त्वानां शान्तिं करोति। मामकीसमाधिना पुष्टिम् । पाण्डरवासिनीसमाधिना रक्षाम् । तारासमाधिना वश्यं करोति। स एव भगवान्रूपवज्रादिका भूत्वा सत्त्वानां सुखसौमनस्य-
A6a मापादयति। स एव भगवान्क्षितिगर्भादिबोधिसत्त्वसमाधिभिः सत्त्वानामायतनविशुद्धिं करोति। स एव भगवान् यमान्तकादिक्रोधसमाधिभिर्दशदिग्विघ्नगणांस्तर्जयति ।

[u]सर्वयोगो हि भगवान्वज्रसत्त्वस्तथागतः ।
तस्योपभोगं सर्वं वै त्रैधातुकमशेषतः ॥[u]

इति वचनात् । मण्डलराजाग्री नाम द्वितीयः समाधिः ॥

TD203b3 TP176b6 [V.1] एवं द्वात्रिंशद्देवताचक्रमभिनिर्माय सूक्ष्मयोगं बाह्याध्यात्मिकजापं

---

[u] **Ce** SBS P166a6

---

1 **sattvānāṃ** AG (sems can rnams kyi T) : om. B ○ °**kleśa**° AG (ñon moṅs pa T) : °**rāga**° B 2 **evaṃ** G; **evam** A (de bźin du T) : om. B 4 **īrṣyā**° G (phrag dog T) : **īrṣā**° A; **mṛṣā**° B 5 **satvānāṃ** AG (sems can rnams kyi T) : om. B; nad la sogs pa add. T 6 **puṣṭiṃ** A (rgyas pa T) : **rakṣāṃ** BG ○ **pāṇḍaravāsinī**° AG : **pāṇḍarā**° B ○ **rakṣāṃ** A (sruṅ ba T) : **puṣṭiṃ** BG 7 °**ādikā** BG : °**ādiko** A 8 de bźin du add. T ○ °**ādi**° AB : °**ādika**° G 11 **sarvayogo** BG : **sarvayogā** A ○ bcom ldan rdo rje T for bhagavat 12 **vai** BG : **vai netuṃ** A 13 samādhiḥ AG : samādhi' B 14 devatā n.e. T ○ **bāhyā‹dhyā›tmikajāpañ** B (phyi naṅ gi bdag ñid can gyi bzlas pa T) : **bāhyādhyātmikajapaṃ** A; **vāgjāpaṃ** G

च कृत्वा पुनरात्मानमेव तथतायां प्रवेशयेत् । ततो B6 लोचनादिच-
तुर्देव्यो G1 मण्डलमध्ये महासुखमपश्यन्त्यो विरहखेदवशात् त्वं वज्र- G18b
चित्तेत्यादिगीतिकाभिर्महासुखं प्रबोधयन्ति। B1 तत्रेयं गीतिका — B12b

[V] त्वं वज्रचित्त भुवनेश्वर सत्त्वधातो
त्रायाहि मां रतिमनोज्ञ महार्थकामैः ।
कामाहि मां जनक सत्त्वमहाग्रबन्धो A3 G2
यदीच्छसे B2 जीवितु मह्य नाथ ॥

त्वं वज्रकाय बहुसत्त्वप्रियाङ्कचक्र
बुद्धार्थ बोधिपरमार्थ हितानुदर्शी ।
रागेण रागसमयां मम कामयस्व
यदीच्छसे जीवितु B3 मह्य नाथ ॥

त्वं वज्रवाच सकलस्य हितानुकम्पी
लोकार्थकार्यकरणे G3 सद सम्प्रवृत्त।

[V] **Cee** GST 17.72–75

---

1 eva n.e. T 3 prabodhayanti AG : prabodhaya{ya}nti B 4 sems can khams na T for sattvadhāto 6 sems can yab chen gñen mchog T for janaka sattvamahāgrabandho 7 yadīcchase BG : yadi¦cchensa¦ A ○ de riṅ ... gson par mchis T for jīvitu mahya; cf. jīvitum adya GST; jīvatu mahya Pi 202 8 bka' yi 'khor lo sems can kun la phan T for bahusattvapriyāṅkacakra 10 **kāmayasva** BG (dgyes par mdzad du gsol T) : **kuryād** A 11 de riṅ ... gson par mchis T for jīvitu mahya; cf. jīvitum adya GST; jīvatu mahya Pi 203 12 sems can kun la T for sakalasya 13 saṃpravṛtta AG; saṃpravṛtt{i}a B

कामाहि मां सुरतचर्य समन्तभद्र
यदीच्छसे जीवितु मह्य [B4] नाथ ॥

त्वं वज्र [A4] काम समयाग्र महाहितार्थ
सम्बुद्धवंशतिलकः समतानुकम्पी ।
कामाहि मां गुणनिधिं बहुरत्नभूतां [G4]
यदीच्छसे [B5] जीवितु मह्य नाथ ॥[v]

TD204a2 TP177a5 [V.2] एवं सद्भूतगुणेन सञ्चोदिते सति पूर्वप्रणिधानसामर्थ्याद्व्युत्थितस्य तथागताश्चाक्षोभ्येत्यादिस्तोत्रराजैः स्तुवन्ति। [B6] तत्रेयं स्तुतिः —

[w]अक्षोभ्यवज्र महाज्ञान [G5] वज्रधातु महाबुध ।
त्रिमण्डल [A5] त्रिवज्राग्र भाष गुह्यं नमो ऽस्तु ते ॥

B13a वैरोचन महाशुद्ध [B1] वज्रशान्त महारते ।

---

[w] **Cee** GST 17.1–5

---

[1] **suratacarya** AG (GST) : **suratacakra** B; spyod pa dri med T for suratacarya ◦ samantabhadra BG : samantadra[!] A [2] de riṅ ... gson par mchis T for jīvitu mahya; cf. jīvitum adya GST; jīvatu mahya Pi 204 [5] °**bhūtāṃ** BG (gyur T) : °**nibhāṃ** A; yon tan rin chen maṅ po'i gter gyur T for guṇanidhiṃ bahuratnabhūtāṃ [6] yadīcchase G; y{ā}adīcchase B : yadi[!]cchase A ◦ de riṅ ... gson par mchis T for jīvitu mahya; cf. jīvitum adya GST; jīvatu mahya Pi 205 [8] **tathāgatāś** AB : **tathāgataś** G ◦ **akṣobhyetyādistotrarājai<ḥ>** em. (mi bskyod pa źes bya ba la sogs pa'i stod pa'i rgyal po rnams kyis T) : **akṣobhyetyādistotrarājai**[!] G; **akṣobhyetyādibhi**[!] **stotrarājai**[!] A; **akṣobhyādisvabhāvena** B ◦ **stuvanti** AG : **saṃstuvanti sma** B [9] mi bskyod pa ni rdo rje che T for akṣobhyavajra mahājñāna; pāda a hypermetrical [10] **trivajrāgra** G (rdo rje mchog gsum T) : **trivajrāgrya** B; **trivajrābhedya** A ◦ **guhyaṃ** B : **guhya** AG; gsaṅ ba'i dbyaṅs la T for bhāṣa guhyam

प्रकृतिप्रभास्वरान्धर्मान् देश वज्र नमो ऽस्तु ते ॥

रत्नराज सुगाम्भीर्य खवज्राकाशनि[G6]र्मल ।
स्वभावशुद्ध निर्लेप भाष गुह्यं नमो ऽस्तु ते ॥

वज्रा[B2]मितमहाराज निर्विकल्प खवज्रधृक् ।
रागपारमिताप्राप्त भाष वज्र नमो ऽस्तु ते ॥

अमोघवज्र सम्बुद्ध सर्वा[A6]शापरिपूरक ।
शुद्धस्वभाव[G7]सम्भूत वज्र[B3]सत्त्व नमो ऽस्तु ते[w]॥

[V.3] तदनन्तरं बुद्धज्ञानं प्रकाश्य मण्डलचक्रमनुराग्य पूर्ववत्स्वकायमण्डले प्रवेश्योपसंहारं कुर्यादनेन क्रमेण। [B4] स्वहृदयस्थं हूंकारमुच्चार्य तेन सकलसत्त्व[G8]धातून्महावज्रधररूपपरिणतान्विचिन्त्य तन्मनसिकारेण विह[B5]रेदिति। अस्य सूत्रं [A1]दशमपटले — TD204a6 TP177b1 A6b

[x]आकाशधातुमध्यस्थं भावयेद्व्यूहमण्डलम् ।

---

[x] **Cee** GST 10.5

---

[1] raṅ bźin gyis ni 'od gsal mchog T for prakṛtiprabhāsvarān dharmān ○ ston pa rdo rje T for deśa vajra [3] **guhyaṃ** B : **guhya** A; **vajra** G; gsaṅ ba'i dbyaṅs la T for bhāṣa guhyam [4] **vajrāmita°** G (rdo rje dpag med T) : **vajrāmṛta°** AB ○ **khavajradhṛk⁰** AB : **khavajriṇaḥ** G [5] rdo rje gsuṅ la T for bhāṣa vajra [8] cakra n.e. T [9] **praveśyopa°** A; **praveśya upa°** B : **anupraveśyopa°** G ○ **krameṇa** AB (rim pa T) : **mantreṇa** G ○ **svahṛdayasthaṃ** AB : **svahṛdistha°** G [10] **uccārya** G; **uccāryya** B : **uccāraya** A ○ **°dhātūn*** BG : **°dhātu** A ○ **°rūpa°** B : **°rūpeṇa** AG ○ **pariṇatān** BG : **pariṇataṃ** A [11] **daśama°** AB : **dvādaśa°** G (le'u bcu gñis pa las T) [12] **vyūha°** AG (bkod pa'i T) : **buddha°** B

हूंकारं तत्र मध्यस्थं स्वबिम्बेन प्रकल्पयेत् ॥

इति ॥

TD204b1 TP177b4 [V.4] एवमादिकर्मिकेण प्रतिष्ठापितसमयसंवरेणाभिषेकप्राप्तेन प्राकृता-
हङ्कारापगतेन चतुःसन्ध्यादेवतायोगाभ्यासेन स्वपरार्थसम्पादनो-
B13b त्सुकेन शान्तिकर्मादिविशिष्टतरमपि कर्तव्यम् । साधनोक्तक्रमेणा-
G19a हारशोधनं कण्ठशोधनं हृदयशोधनं च कृत्वाहारकृत्यं कुर्यात्।
सुखेन परिणमति। बाह्याध्यात्मिकहोमेन त्र्यक्षरेण मालामन्त्रेण वा।
मन्त्रौषधियोगेनापि। पद्मवज्रसमायोगेन च सर्वकर्म प्रसाधयेत् । इति
कर्मराजाग्री नाम तृतीयः समाधिः ॥

श्रीगुह्यसमाजमहायोगतन्त्रे भवोत्पत्तिक्रमेण वज्रसत्त्वनिष्पादनसूत्रं स-
माप्तम् ॥ ॥

कृतिरियमाचार्यचन्द्रकीर्तिपादानाम् ॥ ॥

---

1 **svabimbena prakalpayed** B (GST) : **svabimbe ca prakalpayed** A; **svabimbena parikalpayed** G **4** °**sandhyā**° G : °**sandhya**° A; °**sandhyaṃ** B ○ °**ārthasampādano**° AG (don phun sum tshogs pa T) : °**ārthotpādano**° B **5** **śāntikarmādiviśiṣṭataram** G (źi ba'i las la sogs pa śin tu khyad par can T) : **śāntikādikarmmaprasaram** AB **7** **pariṇamati** BG : **pariṇāmayati** A **8** °**yogenā**° AG : °**saṃyogenā**° B **9** **nāma** AB : om. G **12** **kṛtir iyam ācāryacandrakīrtipādānām** em. : **kṛtir iyaṃ candrakīrtteḥ** A; **kṛtir ācāryacandrakīrttipādānām iti** G; om. B

Tibetan Text

རྒྱ་གར་སྐད་དུ། བཛྲ་ས་ཏྭ་སཱ་དྷ་*ནཾ་ནཱམ། ། D195b6

བོད་སྐད་དུ། རྡོ་རྗེ་སེམས་དཔའི་སྒྲུབ་ཐབས་ཞེས་བྱ་བ། ། N166a7 P168b3 S217b1

N1 དཔལ་འཇམ་པའི་རྡོ་རྗེ་ལ་ཕྱག་P4 འཚལ་ལོ། ། N166b

[I.1] སངས་ རྒྱས་ ཀྱི་ ཐེག་ པ་ མངོན་ པར་ རྟོགས་ པའི་ རིགས་ ཅན་D7 གསུང་ རབ་ འཆད་པའི་དགེ་བའི་བཤེས་གཉེན་དང་ཕྲད་པ་ལས་རྡོ་རྗེ་ཐེག་པར་ཞུགས་ནས་ རྟོག་པ*འི་རྣལ་འབྱོར་*གྱི་ཏིང་ངེ་འཛིན་ལ་སློམས་པར་འཇུག་ཅིང་P5 མཐའ་དྲུག་གི་ བཤད་པ་ལས་ཁ་ཕྱིར་བལྟས་པའི་རྡོ་རྗེ་སློབ་དཔོན་བསྙེན་བཀུར་D1 བྱས་ན་སྒྲ་ཇི་ D196a བཞིན་པའི་དོན་གྱི་སྒོ་ནས་དཔལ་གསང་བ་འདུས་པ་རྣལ་འབྱོར་ཆེན་པོའི་རྒྱུད་ ཐོས་ནས་བྱིས་པས་རྟོགས་པར་བྱ་བའི་དོན་དུ་P6 རྒྱུད་ནས་བཏུས་ནས་ཇི་ལྟར་ཐོབ་ པའི་མན་ངག་གི་རྗེས་སུ་འབྲངས་ནས་རྟོག་*པ་ལྔའི་རྣལ་འབྱོར་D2 གྱི་སྒྲུབ་ཐབས་ལ་ སོགས་པ་སྒྲ་སྣ་ཚོགས་བཀོད་པའི་ཁྱད་པར་*གྱིས་ལུང་རྗེས་སུ་བྱེད་དོ། །

[I.2] དེ་ ལ་ སློབ་ དཔོན་ ཁ་ ཅིག་ ཟླ་ བ་ དང་ རྡོ་ རྗེའི་P7 རིམ་ པས་ རྡོ་ རྗེ་ སེམས་ དཔའ་ རྫོགས་པར་རྟོག་གོ །ཁ་ཅིག་*ནི་སྲིད་པ་སྐྱེ་བའི་རིམ་པས་སོ། །ཁ་ཅིག་ནི་D3 མངོན་ པར་བྱང་ཆུབ་པ་ལྔའི་རིམ་པས་སོ། །ཁ་ཅིག་སྐད་ཅིག་བཞིའི་རིམ་པས་རྡོ་རྗེ་ སེམས་དཔའ་རྫོགས་པར་*རྟོག་གོ །

དཀྱིལ་འཁོར་བའི་ལྷ་P8 ཡང་ཁ་ཅིག་ནི་བཅུ་གསུམ་པར་འདོད་དོ། །ཁ་ཅིག་ནི་བཅུ་ དགུར་འདོད་དོ། །ཁ་ཅིག་ནི་ལྷ་D4 ཉི་ཤུ་རྩ་ལྔར་དགོད་པར་འདོད་དོ། །

---

1 sā dha naṃ D : sā dha nāṃ NPS **6** rtog pa'i NPS : rtogs pa'i D ○ gyi DNP : gyis S **10** rtog pa DNP : rtogs pa S **11** khyad par gyis D : khyad kyis NPS **13** ni D : om. NPS **15** rdzogs par D : om. NPS

དེ་ལྟར་རྒྱུད་འདིར་*རྒྱུ་སྣ་ཚོགས་པ་ལ་བརྟེན་*ནས་རྡོ་རྗེ་སེམས་དཔའ་ལ་སོགས་ [P169a] པ་ལྷའི་སྐུ་རྫོགས་པར་བྱེད་[P1]དོ། །དེའི་རྗེས་སུ་འབྲངས་ནས་ཡང་འགྲེལ་བཤད་ [S218a] དང་། དཀའ་འགྲེལ་[S1]ལ་སོགས་པ་བྱས་[D5]ནས་གདུལ་*བར་བྱ་བའི་སྐྱེ་བོའི་དོན་དུ་སྟོན་པར་བྱེད་དོ། །

དེ་ལ་རྡོ་རྗེ་ཐེག་པ་ལ་མངོན་པར་མོས་པ་དང་དད་པའི་རྗེས་སུ་[P2]འབྲང་བས་དེ་ཁོ་ན་ཉིད་ཀྱི་བརྒྱུད་པ་ཐོབ་ནས། ཐོས་པ་དང་། བསམ་པ་དང་། བསྒོམ་པའི་རིམ་པས་རྫོག་པའི་ལྷའི་རྣལ་[D6]འབྱོར་ལ་གོམས་པར་བྱེད་དོ། །

[I.3] དོན་གྱི་དབང་འདི་དག་རྟོགས་ནས་བདག་གིས་འཕགས་པ་དཔལ་ཀླུ་སྒྲུབ་ཀྱི་[P3]ཞལ་སྔ་ནས་ཀྱི་བརྒྱུད་པ་ལས་འདུས་པ་བཤད་པའི་རྒྱུད་ཀྱི་རྗེས་སུ་འབྲངས་པའི་མཐའ་དྲུག་གི་བཤད་པའི་སྒོ་ནས་རྒྱུད་ཐོས་ཤིང་རིམ་[D7]པ་གཉིས་རྟོགས་ནས། [N167a] སྣ་[N1]ཚོགས་པའི་བསྐྱེད་པའི་རིམ་པ་ལ་མངོན་པར་ཞེན་པ་རྣམས་ཀྱི་རིམ་[P4]པའི་སྒྲུབ་པའི་ཐབས་ལ་ཐེ་ཚོམ་མེད་པར་བྱ་བའི་དོན་དུ། རྡོ་རྗེ་སེམས་དཔའ་བསྐྱེད་པ་ནས་ [D196b] ལེའུ་བཅུ་བདུན་པ་ལ་ཐུག་པ་མདོ་རིམ་པར་བཏུས་ཤིང་བསྡུ་[D1]བར་བྱའོ། །

[II.1] དེ་ལ་རེ་ཞིག་སྒྲུབ་པའི་རིམ་པ་བསྟན་ཏེ།

སྔགས་ཀྱི་ངེས་པ་དང་[P5]པོ་སྟེ། །
གཉིས་པ་དགོད་པ་བསྟན་པའོ། །
རྣམ་པར་བཞག་པ་ཡང་གསུམ་སྟེ། །
བཞི་པ་དེ་ཉིད་བསྟན་པའོ། །

---

1 rgyu NPS : rgyud D ○ brten nas DN : rten nas PS 3 gdul bar D : 'dul bar NPS

ཞེས་བྱ་བའི་རིམ་པས་སྒྲུབ་པའི་ཐབས་ཐོས་ནས། རྡོ་རྗེ་བླ་མའི་གནང་བ་ཐོབ་ནས་རང་གི་འདོད་པའི་ལྷའི་མདུན་དུ་ D2 ཨརྒྷ་ཕུལ་ P6 ཏེ། དེ་ནས་སྒྲུབ་པ་པོས་དགོན་པ་ཆེན་པོ་ལ་སོགས་པའི་ཡིད་དང་རྗེས་སུ་མཐུན་པའི་གནས་སུ་ཤར་དུ་མདོན་པར་ཕྱོགས་པས་སེམས་དཔའི་སྐྱིལ་ཀྲུང་གིས་མཉམ་པར་གནས་ཏེ་སེམས་ཅན་ཐམས་ཅད་ D3 ལ་སྙིང་རྗེ་ཆེན་པོའི་སེམས་ S1 བསྐྱེད་ལ་ P7 འཆད་པར་འགྱུར་བའི་རིམ་ S218b པས་བདག་དང་གཞན་ལ་ཕན་པའི་རྡོ་རྗེ་སེམས་དཔའི་གོ་འཕང་བསྒྲུབ་པར་བྱའོ། །དེའི་དོན་ནི་ལེའུ་བཅུ་གཉིས་པ་ལས།

དགོན་པ་ཆེན་པོའི་ས་ཕྱོགས་ནི། །
མེ་ཏོག་འབྲས་བུ་སོགས་ཀྱིས་བརྒྱན། །
རི་བོ་དབེན་པ་ P8 དག་ D4 ཏུ་ནི། །
དངོས་གྲུབ་ཐམས་ཅད་བསྡུས་པ་འགྲུབ། །

ཅེས་བྱའོ། །

[II.2] དེའི་རྗེས་ལ་སྒྲུབ་པ་པོས་སྟོང་པ་ཉིད་དུ་མོས་པས་ཐ་མལ་པའི་ང་རྒྱལ་བསལ་ལ་སྐད་ཅིག་གིས་བདག་ཉིད་རྡོ་རྗེ་འཆང་ཆེན་པོའི་གཟུགས་སུ་ཁ་དོག་དཀར་པོར་ P1 ལྷག་པར་མོས་པར་བྱའོ། །འདིའི་མདོ་ནི་ལེའུ་གསུམ་པ་ལས། P169b

D5 ནམ་མཁའི་ཁམས་ཀྱི་དབུས་གནས་པར། །
སངས་རྒྱས་དཀྱིལ་འཁོར་བསྒོམ་པར་བྱ། །

2 argha em. : arga D; argā NPS 5 bskyed DS : skyed NP 6 dpa'i D : dpa' NPS ○ bsgrub DNS : sgrub P 7 las DNS : la P

འོད་ཟེར་སྤྲིན་གྱི་ཚོགས་ཆེན་པོ། །
སངས་རྒྱས་འབར་*བར་འདུ་བའི་[P2]འོད། །

ཅེས་བྱའོ། །

[II.3] དེ་ནས་ལེའུ་དང་པོ་ལས་གསུངས་པ། ཡེ་ཤེས་སྒྲོན་*མ་རྡོ་རྗེའི་ཏིང་ངེ་འཛིན་གྱི་ཚུལ་གྱིས་བཛྲ་ཛྙིཀ་ཅེས་བྱ་བའི་སྔགས་[D6]བརྗོད་ལ། དེས་མི་བསྐྱོད་པའི་སྐུ་ནག་ N167b པོ་[N1]ཞལ་གསུམ་པ། ཕྱག་དྲུག་པ། བདག་ཉིད་[P3]ཀྱི་མདུན་དུ་གནས་*པར་བལྟས་ནས། བདག་ཉིད་ཀྱི་ལུས་ལ་ཆུ་དང་འོ་མའི་ཚུལ་གྱིས་རྗེས་སུ་ཞུགས་པས་བདག་ཉིད་ཨིནྡྲ་ནཱིལའི་མདོག་ཅན་ཞེ་སྡང་རྡོ་རྗེའི་སྐུར་བསྒོམས་ཏེ། འདིའི་མདོ་ནི་[D7]ལེའུ་དང་པོ་ལས། དེ་བཞིན་གཤེགས་པ་[P4]ཐམས་ཅད་ཀྱི་སྐུ་དང་། གསུང་དང་། ཐུགས་རིག་པའི་སྐྱེས་བུ་མི་བསྐྱོད་པའི་ཕྱག་རྒྱ་ཆེན་པོར་སྦྱོར་བའི་གོ་ S219a འཕང་མཆོག་གིས་ནག་པོ་[S1]དཀར་པོ་དམར་པོའི་རྣམ་*པས་དེ་བཞིན་གཤེགས་པ་ D197a ཐམས་ཅད་ཀྱི་སྐུ་དང་། གསུང་[P5]དང་། ཐུགས་རྡོ་རྗེའི་དེ་[D1]བཞིན་གཤེགས་པ་ཐམས་ཅད་ཀྱི་སྐུ་དང་། གསུང་དང་། ཐུགས་རྡོ་རྗེ་ལ་*བཞུགས་ཏེ་ཞེས་བྱའོ། །

[II.4.1] དེ་བཞིན་དུ་ཞེ་སྡང་རྡོ་*རྗེའི་ཏིང་ངེ་འཛིན་ལ་གནས་ནས་སྔགས་པས་ཧཱུྃ་རིང་པོ་བརྗོད་*ལ་དེས་བསྐྱེད་པའི་གཤིན་རྗེ་[P6]གཤེད་ལ་སོགས་པ་ཁྲོ་བོ་བཅུ་ཞལ་གསུམ་པ། ཕྱག་དྲུག་[D2]པ། མཚོན་ཆ་སྣ་ཚོགས་པས་བྲེལ་པའི་ཕྱག་ཅན། ཕྱོགས་བཅུ་ན་རྣམ་པར་གནས་པའི་གདུག་པ་ལ་བསྡིགས་པར་བརྩོན་པའི་རྣམ་པར་བསམ་པར་བྱའོ། །འདིའི་མདོ་ནི་[P7]ལེའུ་བཅུ་གསུམ་པ་ལས།

2 bar D : bas NPS **4** sgron ma DNP : sgron me S **6** par D : pa NPS **11** rnam pas D : rnam pa yis NPS **13** bźugs D : źugs NPS **14** rdo rje'i D : rdo rje NPS **15** la NPS : nas D

ཁྲོ་བོ་ཞི་སྡང་གནས་ལ་*སྐྱེས། །

རྟག་ཏུ་གསོད་ལ་དོན་དུ་གཉེར། །

སྒྲུབ་པ་D3 མཆོག་གི་ཆོས་ཅན་གྱི། །

གསོད་དོན་གཉེར་བས་འགྲུབ་པར་འགྱུར། །

ཞེས་བྱའོ། །

[II.4.2] དེ་ནས་འོག་ན་གནས་པའི་གནོད་མཛེས་ལས་གནོད་མཛེས་P8 རྒྱལ་པོ་སྤྱིལ་པ་གཉིས་པ་འོངས་ནས་གནོད་མཛེས་ཀྱི་གཟུགས་ཀྱིས་*མདུན་དུ་གནས་ཏེ་བཀའ་ནོད་པར་བསམས་ནས། ལེའུ་D4 བཞི་པ་ལས་གསུངས་པའི་ཧཱུྃ་བཞི་*པའི་སྔགས་ཀྱིས་བཀའ་བསྒོ་སྟེ། ཨོཾ་སུམྦྷ་ནི་སུམྦྷ་ཧཱུྃ། གྲིཧྞ་གྲིཧྞ་ཧཱུྃ། གྲིཧྞ་པ་ཡ་ P170a
གྲིཧྞ་པ་*ཡ་ཧཱུྃ། ཨཱ་ན་ཡ་ཧོ་བྷ་*ག་བན་བི་*དྱཱ་རཱ་ཛ་ཧཱུྃ་ཕཊ། །དེ་ནས་གནོད་མཛེས་ཀྱི་རྒྱལ་པོ་ཕྱོགས་བཅུར་སོང་སྟེ། ལྷ་ལ་སོགས་པའི་བགེགས་ཀྱི་བདག་པོ་རྣམས་ལྕུགས་D5 ཀྱུས་P2 བཀུག་སྟེ་སྐེ་ལ་ཞགས་པས་བཅིངས་ནས་འོངས་ནས་ཁྲོ་བོ་བཅུ་ལ་སོ་སོར་གཏད་པར་བསམ་པར་བྱའོ། །དེ་ནས་བདུད་རྩི་N1 འཁྱིལ་པ་S1 གཉིས་ N168a S219b
པ་བྱང་ཕྱོགས་ཀྱི་སྒོར་སྤྲུལ་ཏེ་བཞག་ནས་རང་ཉིད་ཕུར་པའི་རྣམ་པ་བཅུ་མངོན་པར་སྤྲུལ་P3 ཏེ་བགེགས་ཀྱི་བདག་པོ་བཅུའི་D6 མགོ་བོར་གནས་པར་བསམ་པར་བྱའོ། །

[II.4.3] དེ་ནས་གནོད་མཛེས་རྒྱལ་པོ་ལངས་ནས་སྔགས་བརྗོད་ཅིང་རྡོ་རྗེ་ཐོ་བས་བརྡུང་བར་བསམ་པར་བྱའོ། །དེ་ལ་སྔགས་ནི་འདི་ཡིན་ཏེ། ཨོཾ་ཧཱ་ཧཱ་ཧཱུ་ཏ་ཡ་ཧཱ་P4

---

1 la D : las NPS   7 kyis D : kyi NPS   9 bźi pa'i D : bźi bźi pa'i NPS
10 gṛhṇā pa ya NPS : gṛhṇa pa ya D ∘ bha ga ban S : bha ga bān DNP
∘ bi dyā rā dza em. : bi dyā rā dzā ya D; bi dya rā dza ya NPS

ཏ་ཡ། སརྦ་དུཥྚཱཾ་ཧཱུཾ་ཧཱུཾ་ཕཊ་ཕཊ། ཀཱི་ལ་ཡ་ཀཱི་ལ་ཡ། སརྦ་པཱ་པཾ་D7ཧཱུཾ་ཧཱུཾ་ཕཊ་ཕཊ། ཧཱུཾ་ཧཱུཾ་ཧཱུཾ་བཛྲ་ཀཱི་ལ་ཡ། བཛྲ་དྷ་ར་ཨཱཛྙཱ་པ་ཡ་*ཏི། སརྦ་དུཥྚཱ་བི་*གྷྣཱ་ནཱཾ་ཀཱ་ཡ་བཱཀྐིཏྟ་*བཛྲཾ་ཀཱི་ལ་ཡ་ཧཱུཾ་ཕཊ། །འདིའི་མདོ་ནི་ལེའུ་བཅུ་གསུམ་པ་P5ལས།

རྡོ་རྗེ་བདུད་རྩི་ཁྲོ་བོ་ཆེ། །
རྡོ་རྗེ་ཕུར་བུ་རབ་བསྒྲིམ་བྱ། །
ཤིན་ཏུ་འབར་ཞིང་ལེགས་པའི་འོད། །
D197b ཕྱོགས་བཅུ་D1འི་རྩེ་མོར་སྤྲོ་བར་བྱ། །

ཞེས་བྱའོ། །

[II.4.4] དེ་ནས་འདོད་པའི་རྒྱལ་པོའི་ཕྱག་རྒྱ་ཀྱི*ས་ལྕགས་དང་། ཆུ་དང་། མེ་དང་། P6རླུང་རྣམས་ཀྱི་ར་བ་བཞི་རིམ་པ་བཞིན་དུ་ཕྱི་རོལ་ཏུ་བསམ་པར་བྱའོ། །དེ་ལ་ཕྱག་ནི་འདི་ཡིན་ཏེ། ཊ་ཀྐི་ཧཱུཾ་*ཛཿ། །དེ་ནས་ཧཱུཾ་གི*ས་སྟེང་དུ་རྡོ་རྗེའི་གུར་མཆོད་རྟེན་ལྟ་བུ་ལྕགས་ཀྱི་ར་བའི་སྟེང་D2དུ་གནས་པའོ། །ཡི་གེ་གསུམ་གྱིས་གོ་ཆ་ལའོ། །P7ཧཱུཾ་གིས་སའི་ཆ་ལ་སྣ་ཚོགས་རྡོ་རྗེའི་ར*ང་བཞིན་དུ་བསམ་པར་བྱའོ། །

[II.4.5] དེ་ལྟར་ཕྱོགས་མཚམས་བཅིང་བ་ནི་རྡོ་རྗེའི་ར་བ་དང་། གུར་ལ་སོགས་པའི་ཚོ་ག་སྔོན་དུ་འགྲོ་བའི་སྲུ*ང་བའི་འཁོར་ལོ་བསམ་པར་བྱའོ། །འདིའི་ཕནD3་ཡོན་གྱི་P8མདོ་ནི་ལེའུ་བཅུ་གསུམ་པ་ལས།

བསམ་གཏན་གང་གིས་ཡི་དམ་ནི། །

---

2 ā dzñā pa ya ti D : a dzñā pa ya ti NPS ○ sarba duṣṭa bighnānāṃ em. : sarba duṣṭāṃ bighnāṃ D; sarbaduṣṭāṃ bighānāṃ NPS 3 badzraṃ em. : badzra DNPS 9 kyis DNP : kyi S 11 dzaḥ D : dza NPS ○ gis em. : gi DNPS 13 raṅ DNS : rab P 15 sruṅ D : bsruṅ NPS

གནས་གང་དུ་ནི་མཚམས་སྦྱོད་པ། །
བསམ་གཏན་སྦྱོར་བ་འདི་ཡིས་ནི། ། S220a
གནས་ནས་སངས་རྒྱས་བྱིན་གྱིས་རློབ། །

ཅེས་བྱའོ། །

[II.4.6] དེ་ ནས་ ལེའུ་ གཉིས་ པ་ལས་ གསུངས་ པའི་ བྱང་ ཆུབ་ སེམས་ ཀྱི་ ཚིགས་བཅད་ཀྱིས་སྲུང་བའི་འཁོར་ལོ་དང་། ཁམས་གསུམ་ཡང་དེ་བཞིན་ཉིད་དུ་གཞུག་པར་བྱའོ། །དེ་ལ་ཚིགས་བཅད་འདི་ཡིན་ཏེ། ། P170b

དངོས་པོ་མེད་པ་སྒོམ་དུ་མེད། ། N168b
བསྒོམ་པར་བྱ་བ་བསྒོམ་པ་མེད། །
དེ་ལྟར་དངོས་དང་དངོས་མེད་པའི། །
བསྒོམ་པ་དམིགས་སུ་མེད་པའོ། །

ཞེས་བྱའོ། །འདི་ཡང་དོན་དམ་པའི་སྲུང་བའོ། །

[II.5.1] དེ་ནས་ནམ་མཁའི་ཁམས་ཀྱི་དབུས་སུ་ཡཾ་ལས་གཞུའི་རྣམ་པའི་རླུང་གི་དཀྱིལ་འཁོར་ཏེ། ཧཱུྃ་གཉིས་ཀྱིས་ལོགས་གཉིས་ལ་རྡོ་རྗེ་གཉིས་ཀྱིས་མཚན་པ་བསམས་ནས་དེའི་སྟེང་དུ་རཾ་ལས་མེའི་དཀྱིལ་འཁོར་གྲུ་གསུམ་པ་རྡོ་རྗེ་གཉིས་ཀྱིས་མཚན་པའོ། །དེའི་སྟེང་དུ་བཾ་ལས་ཆུའི་དཀྱིལ་འཁོར་ཟླུམ་པོ་རྡོ་རྗེ་གཉིས་ཀྱིས་མཚན་པའོ། །དེའི་སྟེང་དུ་ལཾ་ལས་སའི་དཀྱིལ་འཁོར་གྲུ་བཞི་པ་རྡོ་

6 kyis DNP : kyi S ○ : sruṅ ba'i D; bsruṅ ba'i NP; gsuṅs pa'i S
9 bsgom DN : sgom PS **12** sruṅ DNS : bsruṅ P **14** kyis em. : kyi DNPS

རྗེ་གཉིས་ཀྱིས་མཚན་པ་བསམས་ནས། དཀྱིལ་འཁོར་བཞི་ཆར་བསྡུས་པ་ལས་སའི་དཀྱིལ་འཁོར་འབར་ཞིག་ D7 བསམ་ P5 མོ། །འདིའི་མདོ་ནི་ལེའུ་བཅུ་གཅིག་པ་ལས།

དཀྱིལ་འཁོར་རྡོ་རྗེ་ཀུན་ལས་སྐྱེས། །
ནམ་མཁའི་ཁམས་ཀྱི་དབུས་གནས་བསམ། །
དེར་ནི་*ཧྲཱུྃ་ཡིག་བསྒོམ་པར་བྱ། །
རྡོ་རྗེའི་སྤྲིན་ནི་མཉམ་འགྲོ་འོ། །

D198a [II.5.2] དེ་ལྟར་རྟེན་གྱི་དཀྱིལ་འཁོར་བཞི་ P6 བསྐྱེད་ནས། *ཧྲཱུྃ་ལས་ D1 གཞལ་ཡས་ཁང་པ་སྟེ།

གྲུ་བཞི་པ་*ལ་སྒོ་བཞི་པ། །
རྟ་བབས་བཞི་ཡིས་རབ་བརྒྱན་ནས། །
S220b S1 ཐིག་ལེ་བཞི་དང་ཡང་དག་ལྡན། །
ཀ་བ་བརྒྱད་ཀྱིས་ཉེར་བརྒྱན་པ། །

དྲ་བ་དྲ་བ་ཕྱེད་པས་སྤྲས། །
རྡོ་རྗེ་ནོར་བུ་ P7 ཟླ་ཕྱེད་དང་། །
སྒོ་དང་སྒོ་ཁྱུད་མཚམས་རྣམས་སུ། །
D2 རྡོ་རྗེ་རིན་ཆེན་རྣམས་ཀྱིས་བརྒྱན། །

6 bhrūṃ D : bhruṃ NPS **8** bhrūṃ D : bhrum. NPS **10** la DNP : las S

བུམ་པ་ཀ་བ་རྡོ་རྗེ་ཆེ། །
མདའ་ཡབ་དང་ནི་དྲྭ་ཅན་དང་། །
བ་དན་དྲིལ་བུར་ལྡན་པ་ཡི། །
རྟ་ཡབ་སོགས་ཀྱིས་ཉེར་བརྒྱན་པའོ། །

འདིའི་དོན་ནི་ལེའུ་བརྒྱད་པ་ལས།

དཔག་ཚད་བརྒྱ་ཡི་ཁྱོན་ཙམ་ལ། །
ལེགས་པར་མཛེས་ཤིང་གྲུ་བཞི་པ། །
རིན་ཆེན་བཞི་D3དངོས་མཆོད་རྟེན་འདྲ། །
གསལ་ཞིང་རང་བཞིན་དྲི་མེད་པའོ། །

[III.1.1] དེ་ལྟ་བུའི་ལྷ་དང་མི་ལས་ཡོན་ཏན་ཁྱད་པར་དུ་འཕགས་པའི་ཁང་P1 P171a བཟངས་དམ་པ་སའི་དཀྱིལ་འཁོར་གྱི་སྟེང་དུ་བསམས་ཤིང་ཟླ་བ་དང་ཉི་མའི་གདན་རྣམ་པར་བཀོད་ནས། བདག་གི་རང་བཞིན་གྱིས་ཐ་མལ་པའི་ང་རྒྱལ་བས*ལN1་ལ་D4སྐད་ཅིག་གིས་བདག་ཉིད་རྡོ་རྗེ་འཆང་ཆེན་པོའིP2་གཟུགས་ཨིནྡྲ་ N169a *ནཱིལའི་མདོག་ཅན་ཞལ་གསུམ་ཕྱག་དྲུག་པ། གཡས་ཀྱིས་རྡོ་རྗེ་དང་འཁོར་ལོ་དང་པདྨ། གཡོན་གྱིས་དྲིལ་བུ་དང་ཡིད་བཞིན་གྱི་ནོར་བུ་དང་རལ་གྱི་འཛིན་པ། ཁ་སྦྱོར་གྱི་སྦྱོར་བས་དཀྱིལ་འཁོར་གྱི་དབུས་སུ་པདྨ་དང་P3ཉི་མའིD5་གདན་ལ་སེམས་དཔའི་སྐྱིལ་ཀྲུང་གི*ས་ཉེ་བར་གནས་པར་བསམ་མོ། །

[III.1.2] དེ་ནས་ཤར་དུ་རྣམ་པར་སྣང་མཛད། ལྷོར་རིན་ཆེན་འབྱུང་ལྡན། ནུབ་ཏུ་

13 bsal DN : gsal PS   14 nīla'i D : nīla NPS   17 gis DNP : gi S

འོད་དཔག་མེད། བྱང་དུ་དོན་ཡོད་གྲུབ་པའོ། །མེའི་མཚམས་སུ་སྤྱན་མ། བདེན་བྲལ་དུ་མཱ་མ་ཀཱི། རླུང་དུ་གོས་དཀར་མོ། དབང་ལྡན་དུ་སྒྲོལ་མ་རྣམས་སྙིང་པོའི་ S221a དཀྱིལ་འཁོར་བསམས་ནས། རིམ་པ་གཉིས་ལ་མེའི་མཚམས་སུ་གཟུགས་རྡོ་རྗེ་མ། བདེན་བྲལ་དུ་སྒྲ་རྡོ་རྗེ་མ། རླུང་དུ་དྲི་རྡོ་རྗེ་མ། དབང་ལྡན་དུ་རོ་རྡོ་རྗེ་མ། དབུས་སུ་རེག་རྡོ་རྗེ་མ་རྡོ་རྗེ་སེམས་དཔའ་དང་ཡང་དག་པར་འབྲུད་ནས་གནས་པར་བསམ་མོ། །དེ་བཞིན་དུ་རིམ་པ་གསུམ་པའི་ཤར་གྱི་སྣམ་བུ་ལ་བྱམས་པ་དང་སའི་སྙིང་པོ། ལྷོའི་སྣམ་བུ་ལ་ཕྱག་ན་རྡོ་རྗེ་དང་ནམ་མཁའི་སྙིང་པོ། ནུབ་ཀྱི་སྣམ་བུ་ལ་འཇིག་རྟེན་དབང་ཕྱུག་དང་འཇམ་པའི་དབྱངས། བྱང་གི་སྣམ་བུ་ལ་ D198b སྒྲིབ་པ་ཐམས་ཅད་རྣམ་པར་སེལ་བ་དང་ཀུན་ཏུ་བཟང་པོ། ཤར་གྱི་སྒོར་གཤིན་རྗེ་གཤེད་པོ། ལྷོའི་སྒོར་གཞན་གྱིས་མི་ཐུབ་པ། ནུབ་ཀྱི་སྒོར་རྟ་མགྲིན། བྱང་གི་སྒོར་བདུད་རྩི་འཁྱིལ་པ། མེ་མཚམས་སུ་མི་གཡོ་བ། བདེན་བྲལ་དུ་འདོད་པའི་རྒྱལ་པོ། རླུང་དུ་དབྱུག་པ་སྔོན་པོ། དབང་ལྡན་དུ་སྟོབས་པོ་ཆེ། སྟེང་དུ་གཙུག་ཏོར་འཁོར་ལོས་སྒྱུར་བ། འོག་ཏུ་གནོད་མཛེས་རྒྱལ་པོ་བསམ་མོ། །འདིའི་མདོ་ནི་ལེའུ་དང་པོ་ལས།

གསལ་བ་དེ་ཡི་ངོ་བོ་ཉིད། །
ཀུན་ནས་སྣ་ཚོགས་གཟུགས་ལྡན་པར། །
སངས་རྒྱས་སྤྲིན་དང་ཡང་དག་ལྡན། །
འོད་ཟེར་འབར་ཞིང་འཁྲུག་པ་པོ། །
P171b N169b གསལ་བ་ལ་སོགས་དཀྱིལ་འཁོར་ལྡན། །

13 sgyur D : bsgyur NPS ○ bsam mo DNP : bsams mo S ○ mdo D : don NPS **18** 'khrug NPS : 'khrugs D

D3 དེ་བཞིན་གཤེགས་པ་ཀུན་གྱི་གནས། །

ཤེ*ས་བྱའོ། །

[III.1.3] དེ་ལྟར་ཕྱི་རོལ་གྱི་དཀྱིལ་འཁོར་དུ་ལྷ་སུམ་ཅུ་རྩ་གཉིས་སྤྲུལ་པར་མོས་པར་བྱས་ནས། ཡང་འདི་རྣམས་རང་གི་ལུས་ཀྱི་དཀྱིལ་འཁོར་ལ་ཕུང་P2་པོའི་རང་བཞིན་གྱི*ས་སངས་རྒྱས་ལྔ་དང་། ཁམས་ཀྱི་S1་རང་བཞིན་རིག་པའི་ལྷ་མོ་ S221b རྣམས་དང་། D4 སྐྱེ་མཆེད་ཀྱི་རང་བཞིན་གྱི*ས་བྱང་ཆུབ་སེམས་དཔའ་རྣམས་དང་། ཡན་ལག་གི་རང་བཞིན་གྱི*ས་ཁྲོ་བོའི་རྒྱལ་པོ་རྣམས་རྣམ་པར་དགོད་པར་P3་བྱའོ། །
འདིའི་མདོ་ནི་ལེའུ་བཅུ་བདུན་པ་ལས།

ཕུང་པོ་ལྔ་ནི་མདོར་བསྡུས་ན། །
སངས་རྒྱས་ལྔར་ནི་རབ་ཏུ་གྲགས། །
རྡོ་རྗེ་སྐྱེ་མཆེད་ཉིད་ཀྱང་ནི། །
བྱང་ཆུབ་D5་སེམས་དཔའི་དཀྱིལ་འཁོར་མཆོག །

ས་ནི་སྤྱན་མ་ཞེས་སུ་གྲགས། །
P4 ཆུ་ཁམས་མཱ་མ་ཀཱི་རུ་དྲན། །
མེ་ནི་གོས་དཀར་མོ་ཞེས་བྱ། །
རླུང་ནི་སྒྲོལ་མར་རབ་ཏུ་གྲགས། །

གཟུགས་དང་སྒྲ་ལ་སོགས་པ་ཡིས། །
ལྷ་ཉིད་དུ་ནི་རྟག་ཏུ་བསྒོམ། །

---

2 śes NPS : źes D   5 gyis D : gyi NPS   6 gyis NPS : gyi D   7 gyis NPS : gyi D

ཞེས་གསུངས་སོ། །དོན་གྱི་དབང་འདི་D6མཁྱེན*་ནས་སངས་རྒྱས་P5ཐམས་ཅད་དང་མཉམ་པར་སྦྱོར་བ་མཁའ་འགྲོ་མ་དྲ་བ་སྡོམ་པ་རྣལ་འབྱོར་ཆེན་པོའི་རྒྱུད་ལས། བཅོམ་ལྡན་འདས་ཀྱིས་གསུངས་པ།

དེ་ཉིད་མི་སེམས་རྣལ་འབྱོར་བདག །
ལྷ་ཉིད་དུ་ནི་དམིགས་པ་ཡི། །
གཟུགས་བརྙན་རང་P6བཞིན་རྣལ་འབྱོར་ནི། །
ལུགས་D7མ་སོགས་ལས་སྐྱེ་འགྱུར་རམ། །

དེ་ཉིད་ལེགས་སེམས་རྣལ་འབྱོར་ལ། །
ལྷ་རུ་དམིགས་པས་ཅི་ཞིག་བྱ། །
བདག་ཉིད་སྦྱོར་བའི་དམ་ཚིག་ལས། །
མི་འགྱུར་མཆོག་ནི་འགྲུབ་པར་འགྱུར། །

P7བདག་ཉིད་སངས་རྒྱས་ཐམས་ཅད་ཉིད། །
ཀུན་གྱི་མཆོག་ཉིད་ཀྱང་ཡིན་ནོ། །
D199a D1དེ་བས་འབད་པ་ཐམས་ཅད་ཀྱིས། །
བདག་ཉིད་རྟག་ཏུ་མཆོད་པར་བྱ། །

ཞེས་གསུངས་སོ། །

[III.1.4] དེ་ལྟར་ཕྱི་རོལ་གྱི་དཀྱིལ་འཁོར་ལུས་ཀྱི་དཀྱིལ་འཁོར་P8ལ་རྗེས་སུ་བཅུག་
S222a ནས། དེ་S1བཞིན་གཤེགས་པ་ཐམས་ཅད་ཀྱི་རྡུལ་ཕྲ་རབ་ལས་གྲུབ་པར་བདག་

1 mkhyen NPS : mkhyon D

ཉིད་ལུས་ཀྱི་D2 དཀྱིལ་འཁོར་ལྷག་པར་མོས་པར་བྱས་ནས། ཡང་སྐུའི་N1 དཀྱིལ་ N170a
འཁོར་གྱི་ལྷ་རྣམས་ཕུང་པོ་དང་P1 ཁམས་དང་སྐྱེ་མཆེད་ཀྱི་རང་བཞིན་རྣམས་རིམ་ P172a
པ་བཞིན་ཐིམ་པས་དོན་དམ་པའི་དཀྱིལ་འཁོར་དུ་གཞུག་སྟེ། ལེའུ་གསུམ་པ་ལས་གསུངས་པའི་ཨོཾ་ཤུདྡྷ་ཛྙཱན་བཛྲ་སྭ་བྷཱ་བ་D3 ཨཱཏྨ་*ཀོ་ཧཾ་ཞེས་བྱ་བའི་སྔགས་ཀྱིས་P2 ཆོས་སྐུར་བརྟན་*པར་བྱའོ། །འདིའི་མདོ་ནི་ལེའུ་བདུན་པ་ལས།

དམ་ཚིག་ལས་བྱུང་ཁུ་བ་ནི། །
འབྲས་བུ་འདོད་པས་ཆོས་བཞིན་བཏུང་། །
དེ་བཞིན་གཤེགས་པའི་ཚོགས་བསད་*ན། །
དངོས་གྲུབ་རབ་མཆོག་འགྲུབ་པར་*འགྱུར། །

[III.1.5] དེ་P3 ལྟར་D4 སྟོང་པ་ཉིད་དུ་དམིགས་པས་ཉོན་མོངས་པའི་དྲི་མ་ཐམས་ཅད་བསལ་ནས། དེ་ནས་བདག་ཉིད་རྡོ་རྗེ་སེམས་དཔའི་ཕྱག་རྒྱ་ཆེན་པོའི་གཟུགས་སུ་བསྐྱེད་པར་བྱ་སྟེ། རིམ་པ་འདིས་དོན་དམ་པའི་བདེན་པ་ལས་ཉི་P4 མའི་དཀྱིལ་འཁོར། དེའི་སྟེང་དུ་ཟླ་བའི་དཀྱིལ་འཁོར། དེའི་སྟེང་*དུ་པདྨ་D5 དམར་པོ་འདབ་མ་བརྒྱད་པའི་སྟེང་དུ་ཨོཾ་ཨཱཿཧཱུཾ་ཞེས་པའི་ཡི་གེ་གསུམ་གོང་ནས་གོང་དུ་*དགོད་དེ་ཐམས་ཅད་*བསྡུས་པ་ལས་ཟླ་བའི་དཀྱིལ་འཁོར་ཡོངས་སུ་P5 རྫོགས་པར་འགྱུར་ཏེ། སེམས་ཙམ་དུ་བསམས་ནས་དེ་*གཉིས་བརྟན་པ་དང་གཡོ་བའི་འགྲོ་བ་ནང་དུ་འདུས་ཏེ། ལེའུ་D6 གསུམ་པ་ལས་གསུངས་པའི་ཨོཾ་*དྷརྨ་དྷཱ་ཏུ་སྭ་བྷཱ་བ་ཨཱཏྨ་*ཀོ་ཧཾ་

---

4 ātma ko D : atma ko NPS **5** brtan par em. : bstan par DNPS **8** na D : nas NPS **9** 'grub par 'gyur D : 'grub 'gyur ro NPS **14** du DN : om. PS **15** dgod D : bkod NPS **16** bsdus DNS : sdus P **17** gñis DNP : ñid S **18** dharma em. : dharmma DNPS ○ ātma ko DPS : atma ko N

S222b ཞེས་བྱ་བའི་རང་གི་སྔགས་ཀྱིས་རང་གི་སེམས་རིན་[P6]པོ་[S1]ཆེ་བརྟན་*པར་བྱ་བ་འདི་ནི་དང་པོའི་རྣལ་འབྱོར་རོ། །

དོན་འདི་གསལ་བར་འཁོར་ལོ་སྡོམ་པ་ལས་གསུངས་ཏེ།

ཡེ་ཤེས་ཙམ་ལ་སྙོམས་འཇུག་པ། །
རྣལ་[D7]འབྱོར་ཞེས་ནི་མངོན་པར་བརྗོད། །

ཅེས་བྱའོ། །

[III.2] དེ་ནས་ཟླ་བའི་[P7]དཀྱིལ་འཁོར་གྱི་སྟེང་དུ་ཡི་གེ་གསུམ་མོ། ། དེ་ལས་རྡོ་རྗེའོ། ། རྡོ་རྗེ་ལས་བདག་ཉིད་རྡོ་རྗེ་འཆང་ཆེན་པོ་སྐུ་ཁ་དོག་དཀར་པོར་*བསམ་མོ། །

རྡོ་རྗེ་སེམས་དཔའ་རྒྱལ་པོ་ཆེ། །
D199b རྣམ་པར་སྣང་མཛད་མཚུངས་པའི་[D1]འོད། །

N170b [N1]ཅེས་ལེའུ་བཅོ་[P8]ལྔ་པ་ལས་གསུངས་པའི་ཕྱིར་ཏེ། གཉིས་པ་རྗེས་སུ་རྣལ་འབྱོར་རོ། །

འདིའི་མདོ་ནི་ལེའུ་བཅུ་གཅིག་པ་ལས།

རྡོ་རྗེ་གསུམ་ཡིག་སྔགས་མཆོག་གིས། །
ཕྱག་རྒྱ་ཆེན་པོ་བསྒོམ་པ་ནི། །

[1] brtan D : bstan NPS [8] dkar por D : dkar po NPS

ཡེ་ཤེས་རྡོ་རྗེ་བྱ་བ་སྟེ། །
བྱང་[P1]ཆུབ་ཐམས་ཅད་མཉམ་བསྐྱེད་[D2]པའི། ། [P172b]

ཞེས་གསུངས་སོ། །

[III.3.1] དེ་ལྟར་རྣལ་འབྱོར་དང་རྗེས་སུ་རྣལ་འབྱོར་གྱི་རིམ་པས་*བདག་ཉིད་ལོངས་སྤྱོད་རྫོགས་པའི་སྐུར་བསྐྱེད་ནས། སྲིད་པ་ཐ་མལ་པའི་སེམས་ཅན་གྱི་དོན་གྱི་ཕྱིར་ཕུང་པོ་དང་། [P2]ཁམས་དང་། སྐྱེ་མཆེད་*རྗེས་སུ་ཞུགས་པའི་རིམ་པ་འདིས་བདག་[D3]ཉིད་སྤྲུལ་པའི་སྐུར་བསྐྱེད་པར་བྱའོ། །རིམ་པ་འདི་ཡིན་ཏེ། རྣམ་པར་སྣང་མཛད་ཀྱི་རང་བཞིན་ཨོཾ་དཀར་པོ་སྤྱི་བོར་བཀོད་ནས་གཟུགས་ཀྱི་ཕུང་པོ་ལ་གཞུག་[P3]པར་བྱའོ། །འོད་དཔག་ཏུ་མེད་པའི་རང་བཞིན་ཨཱཿདམར་པོ་མགྲིན་པར་བཀོད་ནས་འདུ་ཤེས་ཀྱི་[D4]ཕུང་པོ་ལ་གཞུག་པར་བྱའོ། །མི་བསྐྱོད་པའི་རང་བཞིན་ཧཱུྃ་ནག་པོ་སྙིང་གར་བཀོད་ནས་རྣམ་པར་ཤེས་[S1]པའི་ཕུང་པོ་ལ་གཞུག་པར་བྱའོ། [S223a] །[P4]རིན་ཆེན་འབྱུང་ལྡན་གྱི་རང་བཞིན་སྭཱ་སེར་པོ་ལྟེ་བ་ལ་བཀོད་ནས་ཚོར་བའི་ཕུང་པོ་ལ་གཞུག་པར་བྱའོ། །དོན་ཡོད་གྲུབ་པའི་རང་[D5]བཞིན་ཧཱ་ལྗང་*གུ་རྐང་པ་གཉིས་ལ་བཀོད་ནས་འདུ་བྱེད་ཀྱི་ཕུང་པོ་ལ་གཞུག་པར་བྱའོ། །

[III.3.2] མོ་ཧ་ར་ཏི་[P5]ཞེས་བྱ་བས་སྤྱན་མ་སའི་ཁམས་ཀྱི་རང་བཞིན་གྱིས་སོ། །དྭེ་ཥ་ར་ཏི་ཞེས་བྱ་བས་མཱ་མ་ཀཱི་ཆུའི་ཁམས་ཀྱི་རང་བཞིན་གྱིས་སོ། །རཱ་ག་ར་ཏི་ཞེས་བྱ་བས་གོས་དཀར་མོ་[D6]མེའི་ཁམས་ཀྱི་རང་བཞིན་གྱིས་སོ། །བཛྲ་ར་ཏི་ཞེས་བྱ་[P6]བས་སྒྲོལ་མ་རླུང་གི་ཁམས་ཀྱི་རང་བཞིན་གྱིས་སོ། །བཀོད་ནས་སྲ་བ་ཉིད་དང་། གཤེར་བ་ཉིད་དང་། དྲོ་བ་ཉིད་དང་། གཡོ་བ་ཉིད་དུ་རབ་ཏུ་བསམ་པར་

4 pas D : pa NPS   6 skye mched NPS : skye mched daṅ D   13 ljaṅ gu D : ljaṅ khu NPS

བྱའོ། །

[III.3.3] ཨོཾ་སའི་སྙིང་པོའི་*ས་བོན་མིག་གི་སྐྱེ་མཆེད་ཀྱི་རང་བཞིན་[D7]དང་། [P7]ཨོཾ་ཕྱག་ན་རྡོ་རྗེའི་ས་བོན་རྣ་བའི་སྐྱེ་མཆེད་ཀྱི་རང་བཞིན་དང་། ཨོཾ་ནམ་མཁའི་སྙིང་པོའི་ས་བོན་སྣའི་སྐྱེ་མཆེད་ཀྱི་རང་བཞིན་དང་། N171a ཨོཾ་[N1]འཇིག་རྟེན་དབང་ཕྱུག་གི་ས་བོན་ལྗེའི་སྐྱེ་མཆེད་རང་བཞིན་དང་། ཧཱུཾ་འཇམ་དཔལ་གྱི་ས་བོན་[P8]ཡིད་ཀྱི་སྐྱེ་མཆེད་ཀྱི་རང་བཞིན་[D1]དང་། D200a ཨོཾ་སྒྲིབ་པ་ཐམས་ཅད་རྣམ་པར་སེལ་བའི་ས་བོན་ལུས་ཀྱི་སྐྱེ་མཆེད་ཀྱི་རང་བཞིན་ལ་བཀོད་ནས། ལྷའི་མིག་ལ་སོགས་པར་རབ་ཏུ་བརྟག་པར་བྱའོ། །བྱམས་པའི་ས་བོན་མཻཾ་[P1]རྒྱུས་པའི་རང་བཞིན་ལ་དགོད་པར་བྱའོ། P173a །ཀུན་ཏུ་བཟང་པོའི་ས་བོན་[D2]*སཾ་ལུས་ཀྱི་*ཚིགས་ཐམས་ཅད་ལ་དགོད་པར་བྱའོ། །

S223b **[III.3.4]** དེ་ལྟར་སྔགས་ཀྱིས་བྱིན་གྱིས་བརླབས་*པ་ལས་[S1]ཕུང་པོ་དང་། ཁམས་དང་། སྐྱེ་[P2]མཆེད་བཀང་ནས་ཧཱུཾ་རིང་པོ་*ལས་ཁྲོ་བོ་བཅུ་ལག་པ་ལ་སོགས་པའི་ཡན་ལག་རྣམས་ལ་རིམ་པ་འདིས་དགོད་པར་བྱས་ཏེ། དེ་ལ་ལག་པ་གཡས་པར་[D3]གཤིན་རྗེ་གཤེད། ལག་པ་གཡོན་པ་ལ་གཞན་གྱིས་མི་ཐུབ་པ། ཁར་རྟ་[P3]མགྲིན། གསང་བར་ནི་བདུད་རྩི་འཁྱིལ་པ། རྐྱབ་མ་གཡས་པར་མི་གཡོ་བ། གཡོན་པར་འདོད་པའི་རྒྱལ་པོ། པུས་མོ་གཡས་པ་ལ་དབྱུག་སྔོན་*ཅན། པུས་མོ་གཡོན་པ་ལ་སྟོབས་པོ་ཆེ། སྤྱི་[D4]བོར་གཙུག་ཏོར་འཁོར་ལོས་*[P4]སྒྱུར་*བ། རྐང་པ་གཉིས་ལ་གནོད་མཛེས་རྒྱལ་པོ་བཀོད་ནས་ཕྱོགས་བཅུར་རྗེས་སུ་གཞུག་པར་བྱའོ། །འདིའི་མདོ་ནི་ལེའུ་དང་པོ་ལས། རིག་པའི་སྐྱེས་བུ་ཆེན་པོའི་སྐུ་དེ་བཞིན་གཤེགས་པ་ཐམས་ཅད་ཀྱི་[P5]སྔགས་ཀྱིས་*བྱིན་གྱིས་བརླབས་ནས་དེ་མ་

---

2 po'i DNP : po S **9** saṃ D : sam NPS ○ tshigs D : tshogs NPS **10** brlabs DNP : brlab S **11** riṅ po las NPS; riṅ por D **15** can D : om. NPS **16** los D : lo NPS ○ sgyur DNP : bsgyur S **19** kyis D : kyi NPS

ཐག་ཏུ་[D5]བྱིན་གྱིས་བརླབས་པ་ཙམ་གྱིས་བྱང་ཆུབ་ཀྱི་སེམས་རྡོ་རྗེ་དེ་ཉིད་དེ་བཞིན་གཤེགས་པ་རྣམས་ཀྱི་ཞལ་གསུམ་གྱི་རྣམ་པར་མཐོང་བར་གྱུར་ཏོ། །ཞེས་བྱ་བ་*ནི་གསུམ་པ་[P6]ཤིན་ཏུ་རྣལ་འབྱོར་རོ། །

[III.4.1] དེ་ལྟར་སྒྲུབ་པ་པོས་རྣལ་འབྱོར་གསུམ་གྱི་བདག་ཉིད་ཀྱིས་ཐ་མལ་པའི་ང་རྒྱལ་བསལ་ཏེ། [D6]དཔལ་རྡོ་རྗེ་སེམས་དཔའི་སྐུར་ཡང་བསྐྱེད་ནས། ཡང་བྱ་བ་ནི་ཡོངས་སུ་རྫོགས་པའི་ལྷའི་རྣམ་རྟོག་[P7]བསལ་བའི་ཕྱིར་བཞི་པ་རྣལ་འབྱོར་ཆེན་པོ་[N1]བྱ་སྟེ། དེ་ལ་ཨོཾ་ཁ་དོག་དཀར་པོ་སྤྱི་བོར་བསམས་ནས་དེ་ལས་སྐྱེས་པའི་ N171b སྤྱན་གྱི་ཚོགས་བདག་པོའི་སྦྱོར་བས་ནམ་མཁའི་དབྱིངས་སུ་རྣམ་པར་[D7]བསམས་ཏེ། [S1]དེ་ནས་སྐད་[P8]ཅིག་གིས་རྣམ་པར་སྣང་མཛད་ཀྱི་ཚོགས་བདག་པོ་དང་སྦྱོར་ S224a བ་བར་སྣང་ལ་བསམས་ནས། ལེའུ་བཅུ་*གཉིས་པ་ལས་གསུངས་པའི་ཚིགས་བཅད་གཉིས་ཀྱིས་གསོལ་བ་གདབ་པར་བྱའོ། །དེ་ལ་ཚིགས་བཅད་ནི་འདི་ཡིན་ཏེ།

སངས་[P1]རྒྱས་སྐུ་[D1]འཆང་དཔལ་དང་ལྡན། ། P173b D200b
རྡོ་རྗེ་མི་ཕྱེད་གསུམ་བསྒོམས་པས། །
དེང་བདག་བྱིན་གྱིས་བརླབས་ནས་སུ། །
རྡོ་རྗེ་སྐུ་ཡིས་མཛད་དུ་གསོལ། །

རྡོ་རྗེ་མི་ཕྱེད་གསུམ་བསྒོམས་པས། །
ཕྱོགས་བཅུར་བཞུགས་པའི་སངས་རྒྱས་[P2]རྣམས། །
དེང་བདག་བྱིན་བརླབས་གོམས་པ་ནི། །

3 ni D : na NPS   10 bcu gñis pa em. : gñis pa DNPS

རྡོ་རྗེ་སྐུས་D2ནི་མཛད་དུ་གསོལ། །

གསོལ་བ་བཏབ་མ་ཐག་ཏུ་ལྷའི་ཚོགས་ཕན་ཚུན་རྗེས་སུ་ཆགས་པ་སྤྱོན་དུ་འགྲོ་བས་མཆོག་ཏུ་དགའ་བ*འི་བདེ་བ་ཉམས་སུ་མྱོང་བས་འོད་ཟེར་P3དཀར་པོའི་རང་བཞིན་གྱིས་ཡེ་ཤེས་སེམས་དཔའི་རང་བཞིན་དུ་རྣམ་པར་སྣང་མཛད་ཀྱི་སྒོ་ནས་ཞུགས་ནས*་ཡེ་ཤེས་ས*་ཐོབ་D3པས་ལུས་ཐམས་ཅད་བཀང་སྟེ་ཚིམ་པར་བསམས་ནས་ལེའུ་བདུན་པ་ལས་གསུངས་པའི་ཚིགས་སུ་བཅད་པས་P4བསྟན་པར་བྱའོ། །
ཚིགས་སུ་བཅད་པ་འདི་ཡིན་ཏེ།

སངས་རྒྱས་ཀུན་གྱི་སྐུ་གང་གིས། །
ཕུང་པོ་ལྔ་ནི་རབ་བཀང་བ། །
སངས་རྒྱས་སྐུ་ཡི་རང་བཞིན་གྱིས། །
བདག་ཀྱང་དེ་D4དང་འདྲ་བར་ཤོག །

དེ་ནས་ལེའུ་བདུན*་པ་ལས་P5གསུངས་པའི་སྔགས་ཀྱིས་གཉིས་སུ་མེད་པའི་ང་རྒྱལ་བྱ་སྟེ། ཨོཾ་སརྦ་ཏ་ཐཱ་ག་ཏ་ཀཱ་ཡ་བཛྲ་སྭ་བྷཱ་བ་ཨཱཏྨ*་ཀོ྅ཧཾ་ཞེས་བྱ་བས་སོ། །

S224b [III.4.2] སྐུ་དང་གསུང་དང་ཐུགས་ཀྱི་རིམ་པ་འདིས་བྱིན་གྱིས་S1བརླབ་པར་བྱའོ། །
དེ་ལ་རིམ་པ་ནི་P6འདི་ཡིན་ཏེ། ཨཱཿ*D5ཁ་དོག་དམར་པོ་མགྲིན་པའི་པདྨའི་སྟེང་དུ་བཀོད་ནས། དེ་ལས་བྱུང་བའི་གོས་དཀར་མོའི་ཚོགས་ཀྱིས*་ནམ་མཁའ་བཀང་ནས། སྔར་བཞིན་དུ་འོད་དཔག་མེད་ཀྱི་ཚོགས་བལྟས་ནས་ཚིགས་བཅད་འདིས་གསོལ་བ་P7གདབ་པར་བྱའོ། །

---

3 ba'i D : ba NPS **5** źugs nas D : om. NPS ○ sa NPS : om. D **12** bdun pa NPS : drug pa D **13** ātma ko D : atma ko NPS **15** āḥ D : a NPS **16** kyis DNP : kyi S

ཆོས་ཀྱི་གསུང་ལམ་དཔལ་དང་ལྡན། །
[N1] རྡོ་རྗེ་མི་[D6]ཕྱེད་གསུམ་བསྒོམས་པས། ། N172a
དེང་བདག་ཕྱིན་གྱིས་བརླབས་ནས་སུ། །
རྡོ་རྗེ་གསུང་གིས་མཛོད་དུ་གསོལ། །

ཕྱོགས་བཅུར་བཞུགས་པའི་སངས་རྒྱས་རྣམས། །
[P8] རྡོ་རྗེ་མི་ཕྱེད་གསུམ་བསྒོམས་པས། །
དེང་བདག་ཕྱིན་གྱིས་བརླབས་ནས་སུ། །
རྡོ་རྗེ་གསུང་གིས་མཛོད་དུ་གསོལ། །

[D7] དེ་ལྟར་གསོལ་བ་བཏབ་ནས། སྔར་བཞིན་དབང་པོ་གཉིས་མཉམ་པར*་སྦྱོར་བས་འདོད་ཆགས་ཆེན་[P1]པོའི་མེས་ཚོགས་གཉིས་ཞུ་བ་ལས་འོད་ཟེར་དམར་པོའི་ P174a གཟུགས་ཀྱིས་ཞལ་དུ་ཞུགས་པ་ལས་ངག་གི*་དབང་ཕྱུག་ཐོབ་པར་བསམས་ནས། ཚིགས་སུ་བཅད་པ་འདིས་བསྟན་པར་[D1]བྱའོ། ། D201a

གང་ཞིག་རྡོ་རྗེ་ཆོས་ཀྱི་ནི[P2]། །
ངེས་ཚིག་ཕུན་སུམ་ཚོགས་པའི་ངག*། །
བདག་གི་ཚིག་ཀྱང་དེ་འདྲ་ཞིང་། །
ཆོས་འཛིན་པ་དང་འདྲ་བར་ཤོག །

ཅེས་གསུངས་སོ། །ཐུགས་འདིས་གཉིས་སུ་མེད་པའི་རྣམ་པའི་ང་རྒྱལ་བྱ་སྟེ། དེ་

9 mñam par D : sṅar mñam par NPS **11** gi D : gis NPS **14** ṅag NPS : ṅab D

ལ་སྔགས་ནི་འདི་ཡིན་ཏེ། D2 ཨོཾ་སརྦ་P3 ཏ་ཐཱ་ག་ཏ་ཝཱཀ་བཛྲ་སྭ་བྷཱ་ཝ་ཨཱཏྨ་*ཀོ་ཧཾ་ཞེས་བྱའོ། །

[III.4.3] དེ་ནས་ཡང་རང་གི་སྙིང་གའི་རྡོ་རྗེའི་ལྟེ་བར་ཧཱུྃ་ཁ་དོག་ནག་པོ་བསམས་ནས། S225a དེ་ལས་སྤྲོས་པའི་སྨ་མ་ཀླུའི་S1 ཚོགས་ནམ་མཁའ་ལ་བསམས་ཏེ། སྤུ་མ་བཞིན་དུ་སྐད་ཅིག་P4 གིས་མི་བསྐྱོད་པའི་ཚོགས་བར་སྣང་ལ་བཀྲུས་D3 ནས་ཚིགས་སུ་བཅད་པ་འདིས་གསོལ་བ་གདབ་པར་བྱའོ། །

དཔལ་ལྡན་རྡོ་རྗེ་ཐུགས་འཆང་བ། །
རྡོ་རྗེ་མི་ཕྱེད་གསུམ་བསྒོམས་པས། །
དེང་བདག་བྱིན་བརླབས་གསོལ་P5 བ་ནི། །
རྡོ་རྗེ་ཐུགས་ཀྱིས་མཛད་དུ་གསོལ། །

ཕྱོགས་བཅུར་བཞུགས་པའི་སངས་རྒྱས་རྣམས། །
རྡོ་རྗེ་མི་ཕྱེད་D4 གསུམ་བསྒོམས་པས། །
དེང་བདག་བྱིན་བརླབས་གསོལ་བ་ནི། །
རྡོ་རྗེ་ཐུགས་ཀྱིས་མཛད་དུ་གསོལ། །

ཞེས་P6 གསོལ་བ་བཏབ་མ་ཐག་ཏུ་སྔར་བསྟན་པ་བཞིན་དུ་གཉིས་སུ་མེད་པའི་འདོད་ཆགས་ཆེན་པོའི་མེས་ཞུ་བས་འོད་ཟེར་ནག་པོའི་གཟུགས་ཀྱིས་ཐུགས་ཀར་ཞུགས་པས་ཐུགས་ཀྱི་D5 དབང་ཕྱུག་ཐོབ་པར་བསམས་ནས་ཚིགས་སུ་བཅད་P7 པ་འདིས་བསྟན་པར་བྱའོ། །

1 ātma ko em. : atma ko DNPS

ཀུན་ཏུ་བཟང་པོའི་ཕྱགས་ N1 གང་ཡིན། ། N172b
གསང་བའི་དབང་པོ་བློ་ལྡན་པ། །
བདག་ཀྱང་དེ་དང་འདྲ་འགྱུར་ཏེ། །
ཕྱགས་འཛིན་པ་དང་འདྲ་བར་ཤོག །

ཅེས་བྱའོ། །དེ་ནས་ སྤྱགས་འདིས་གཉིས་སུ་མེད་ P8 པའི་རྣམ་ D6 པའི་ང་རྒྱལ་བྱ་སྟེ། ཨོཾ་སརྦ་ཏ་ཐཱ་ག་ཏ་ཙི་ཏྟ་བཛྲ་སྭ་བྷཱ་བ་ཨཱཏྨ་ཀོ྅ཧཾ་ཞེས་བྱའོ། །

[III.4.4] དེ་ལྟ་བུའི་རིགས་གསུམ་བཅུག་པས་སྐུ་གསུང་ཕྱགས་སོ་སོའི་བྱིན་གྱིས་བརླབས་ནས། ཡང་རྡོ་རྗེ་གསུམ་མི་ཕྱེད་པའི་རང་ P1 བཞིན་གྱིས་རྡོ་རྗེ་འཆང་ཆེན་ P174b
པོར་བྱིན་གྱིས་བརླབ་པ་འདིས་བྱའོ། D7 །ཨོཾ་སརྦ་ཏཐཱ་ག་ཏ་ཀཱ་ཡ་ཝཱཀ་ཙིཏྟ་བཛྲ་སྭ་བྷཱ་བ་ཨཱཏྨ་ཀོ྅ཧཾ་ཞེས་བྱའོ། །འདིའི་མདོ་ནི་ལེའུ་ S1 གཉིས་པ་ལས། བཅོམ་ལྡན་ S225b
འདས་སེམས་ལུས་ P2 ཀྱི་རྣམ་པ་དང་། ལུས་སེམས་ཀྱི་རྣམ་པ་དང་། སེམས་ངག་གི་བརྗོད་པའི་རྣམ་པ་ལྟ་བུ་བསྐྱེད་པར་བྱའོ་ཞེས་གསུངས་ D1 སོ། །ལེའུ་དང་པོ་ལས་ D201b
གསུངས་པའི་དམ་ཚིག་ལས་བྱུང་བ་རྡོ་རྗེའི་ཏིང་ངེ་འཛིན་གྱི་ཚུལ་གྱིས་བསྐྱེད་པའི་ P3 ཕྱིར་དམ་ཚིག་སེམས་དཔའ་ཞེས་བརྗོད་དོ། །

[III.4.5] དེ་ལྟར་ཞལ་གསུམ་ཕྱག་དྲུག་པར་དམ་ཚིག་སེམས་དཔའ་བསྐྱེད་ནས། དེའི་སྙིང་གར་ཡེ་ཤེས་སེམས་དཔའ་ཕྱག་གཉིས་པ། D2 མདོག་དམར་པོ་ཁ་སྦྱོར་གྱི་སྦྱོར་བས་ལུས་ P4 ཐམས་ཅད་ཚིམ་པར་བསམས་ནས་རང་གི་ཅོད་པན་ལ་བདག་པོ་བསམ་མོ། །འདིའི་མདོ་ནི་ལེའུ་བཅུ་གཉིས་པ་ལས།

6 ātma ko D : atma ko NPS ○ źes bya'o NPS : źes bya ba'o D 9 por D : po'i NPS ○ brlab D : brlabs NPS ○ bāk DN : bāg PS 10 ātma ko D : atma ko NPS 13 gyis D : om. NPS 17 kha sbyor gyi sbyor bas D : kha sbyor bas NPS

རྣམ་པ་ཀུན་གྱི་མཆོག་ལྡན་པའི། །
བདག་ཉིད་སྐུ་གསུང་ཐུགས་རྡོ་རྗེའི། །
དམ་ཚིག་ཐུགས་ཀར་ཡེ་ P5 ཤེས་དང་། །
D3 རྡོ་རྗེ་མཆོག་འཛིན་ཅོད་པན་ལའོ། །

སངས་རྒྱས་རྣམས་ནི་ཚིམ་བྱེད་པའི། །
དམ་ཚིག་འདི་ནི་དམ་པའོ། །
དམ་ཚིག་ཀུན་གྱི་བྱ་བ་སྟེ། །
དངོས་གྲུབ་ཐམས་ཅད་སྒྲུབ་བྱེད་པ། །

ཞེས་གསུངས་སོ། །དེ་ལྟར་དམ་ཚིག་ P6 སེམས་དཔའི་ཐུགས་ཀར་ཡེ་ཤེས་སེམས་དཔའ་བསམས་ D4 ནས། ཡེ་ཤེས་སེམས་དཔའི་ཐུགས་ཀར་ཡི་གེ་ཧཱུྃ་ཉིད་དེ་འཛིན་སེམས་དཔའ་ཞེས་བྱ་བ་རྟག་ཏུ་འཆར་བ་མར་མེ་ཆེན་པོ་ལྟ་བུ་མི་ཤེས་པའི་མུན་པ་འཇོམས་པའི་དོན་དུ་སྣང་ P7 བའི་ཕུང་པོ་ལྟ་བུ་བསམ་པར་བྱའོ། །འདིའི་མདོ་ནི་ལེའུ་བཅུ་གཅིག་པ་ལས།

N173a སངས་ N1 རྒྱས་དཀྱིལ་འཁོར་ D5 དབུས་གནས་པ། །
S226a མི་བསྐྱོད་རྡོ་རྗེ་རབ་ S1 བསྒོམ་བྱ། །
ཧཱུྃ་ཡིག་སྙིང་གར་བསྒོམས་ནས་ནི། །
སེམས་ནི་ཐིག་ལེར་གནས་པར་ P8 བཞག །

ཅེས་བྱ་བ་ནི་རྣལ་འབྱོར་ཆེན་པོའོ། །

[IV.1] དེ་ལྟར་རྣལ་འབྱོར་བཞིས་བདག་ཉིད་སེམས་དཔའ་གསུམ་གྱི་བདག་ཉིད་ཅན་*གྱི་བདག་*གི་དོན་*ཕུན་[D6]སུམ་ཚོགས་པའི་རང་བཞིན་ཏིང་ངེ་འཛིན་རྒྱལ་པོ་མཆོག་བསྐྱེད་ནས། ད་ནི་[P1]གཞན་གྱི་དོན་*ཕུན་སུམ་ཚོགས་པའི་ཕྱིར་དཀྱིལ་ [P175a] འཁོར་རྒྱལ་པོ་མཆོག་ཅེས་བྱ་བའི་ཏིང་ངེ་འཛིན་*བསྟན་པའི་སྐབས་ལ་འཇུག་པར་བྱ་སྟེ། བཅོམ་ལྡན་འདས་ཤཱཀྱ་ཐུབ་པས་ཐམས་ཅད་མཛད་དེ་[D7]དགའ་ལྡན་གྱི་གནས་མཆོག་[P2]ནས་བབས་ཏེ། ཐམས་ཅད་མཁྱེན་*པར་མཛད་ནས་འདོད་ཆགས་དང་བྲལ་བར་མངོན་པར་སྤྲུལ་ཏེ། ཉན་ཐོས་ཀྱི་རིགས་ཅན་རྣམས་ཉན་ཐོས་ཀྱི་ས་ལ་བཀོད་དོ། །ཡང་ཐེག་པ་ཆེན་པོའི་སེམས་ཅན་རྣམས་ལ་ཕ་རོལ་ཏུ་ཕྱིན་[P3]པའི་ཚུལ་ཐམས་ཅད་[D1]གསལ་བར་མཛད་ནས་ཟབ་མོ་ལ་ལྷག་པར་མོས་པ་རྣམས་ལ་ [D202a] འདོད་ཆགས་ལས་སྐྱེས་པའི་བྱང་ཆུབ་འདི་བསྟན་པའི་དོན་དུ་དེ་ལས་ལེའུ་དང་པོ་ལས་གསུངས་པའི་འདོད་ཆགས་ཆེན་པོའི་ཚུལ་ཞེས་བྱ་བའི་ཏིང་ངེ་འཛིན་དེ་ལ་སྙོམས་པར་ཞུགས་པ་དེ་བཞིན་དུ་སློབ་[D2]བཞིན་པའི་རྣལ་འབྱོར་པས་ཀྱང་དང་པོ་སྦྱོར་བ་བྱས་ནས་འདོད་ཆགས་ལ་སྤྱོད་པའི་སེམས་ཅན་རྣམས་འདོད་པས་ཐར་པར་རབ་ཏུ་བསྟན་པའི་ཕྱིར། ལེའུ་བཅུ་བདུན་པ་ལས་གསུངས་པའི་རིམ་*པ་འདིས་འདོད་པ་ཀུན་*ལ་ལོངས་སྤྱོད་པའི་ཏིང་ངེ་འཛིན་འདི་ཡིས་གནས་པར་བྱ། [D3][P4]།དེ་ལ་རིམ་པ་འདི་ཡིན་ཏེ། མཚན་མ་ཐམས་ཅད་དང་ལྡན་པའི་ཕྱིའི་ཕྱག་རྒྱ་སྔགས་དང་རྒྱུད་ལ་ལེགས་པར་*བསླབས་པ་རྙེད་ནས་མདུན་དུ་བཞག་སྟེ་རིགས་ལྔ་*བརྟག་པར་བྱའོ། །དེ་ནས་རྡོ་རྗེ་པདྨ་འདུས་བྱས་པ་སྔོན་དུ་འགྲོ་བས་[P5]དབང་པོ་གཉིས་མཉམ་དུ་སྦྱར་བར་བྱས་[D4]ནས། བྱང་ཆུབ་[S1]ཀྱི་སེམས་ལས་མི་བསྐྱོད་ [S226b]

2 gyi DNP : gyis S ∘ gi DNP : gis S ∘ phun DNS : phuṅ P **3** phun DNS : phuṅ P **4** bstan DNP : brtan S **6** par NPS : pa D **15** de le'u daṅ po las gsuṅ pa'i ... le'u bcu bdun pa las gsuṅs pa'i rim pa D : om. NPS ∘ la em. : las DNPS **17** bslabs D : brlabs NPS **18** brtag DNP : rtag S

པ་ལ་སོགས་པའི་དཀྱིལ་འཁོར་གྱི་འཁོར་ལོ་མངོན་པར་སྤྲུལ་ཏེ། དེ་དང་དེའི་ཏིང་ངེ་འཛིན་གྱིས་སེམས་ཅན་རྣམས་ཀྱི་ཞེ་སྡང་ལ་སོགས་[P6]པའི་ཉོན་མོངས་པ་སྦྱངས་ནས་ཡང་སླར་བསྡུས་ཏེ། རང་གི་ལུས་ཀྱི་དཀྱིལ་འཁོར་ལ་[D5]གཞུག་པར་
N173b བྱའོ། །ཡང་ན་སྙིང་གར་ཡེ་ཤེས་ཀྱི་ཕྱག་རྒྱ་མངོན་པར་[N]སྤྲུལ་ཏེ། དེ་དང་ལྷན་ཅིག་སྙོམས་པར་འཇུག་པར་[P7]བྱས་ནས་ཐུགས་ཅིག་སྤྲུལ་པས་སེམས་ཅན་གྱི་དོན་བྱའོ། །

སྙིང་གར་གནས་པའི་ལྷ་མོ་ཆེ། །
རྣལ་འབྱོར་རྣལ་འབྱོར་འབེབས་བྱེད་མ། །
སངས་[D6]རྒྱས་རྣམས་ཀྱི་སྤྱོར་སྐྱེད་མ། །
རྡོ་རྗེ་དབྱིངས་ཀྱི་དབང་མོར་གྲགས། །

[P8]ཞེས་བྱ་བ་ཐམས་ཅད་གསང་བའི་རྒྱུད་ལས་གསུངས་པའི་ཕྱིར་རོ། །འདིའི་མདོ་ནི་ལེའུ་བདུན་པ་ལས་གསུངས་པ།

བཙུན་མོ་ཤིན་ཏུ་ཡིད་འོང་མ། །
བཅུ་དྲུག་ལོ་ལོན་རྙེད་ནས་ནི། །
P175b བྱིན་བརླབས་[D7]གོ་འཕང་*་གསུམ་[P1]གྱིས་ནི། །
དབེན་པར་མཆོད་པ་བརྩམ་པར་བྱ། །

དེ་བཞིན་གཤེགས་པའི་བཙུན་མོ་མཆོག །
སྤྱན་མ་རྣམ་པར་བསྒོམ་བྱ་སྟེ། །

---

15 'phaṅ D : 'phaṅs NPS

དབང་པོ་གཉིས་ནི་མཉམ་སྦྱོར་བས། །
སངས་རྒྱས་དངོས་གྲུབ་ཐོབ་པར་བྱེད། །

ཅེས་བྱ*་བ་

[IV.2] དེ་ལྟར་ཕྱི[P2]་ནང་གི[D1]་བདག་ཉིད་ཅན་གྱི་ཕྱག་རྒྱ་ལ་ངེས་པར་བྱས་ནས་རིགས་ D202b ལྔའི་བཏག་པའི་རིམ་པ་བསྟན*་པར་བྱ་སྟེ། ཨོཾ་ནི་སྤྱི་བོར་རོ། །ཨཱཿནི་ཁ་ལའོ། །ཧཱུྃ་ནི་སྙིང་གར་རོ། །སྭཱ་ལྟེ་བར་རོ། །ཧཱ་ཁང་པ་གཉིས་ལ་དགོད་དོ། །ཁམས་བཞིའི[P3]་རང་བཞིན་གྱིས*་སྤྱན[S1]་མ་ལ་སོགས་པ་རྣམས[D2]་དགོད་དོ། །མིག་ལ་སོགས་པའི་ S227a སྐྱེ་མཆེད་ཀྱི་རང་བཞིན་གྱིས*་གཟུགས་རྡོ་རྗེ་མ་ལ་སོགས་པ་དགོད་དོ། །ཡང་དེའི་ལག་པ་ལ་སོགས་པ་ཡན་ལག་རྣམས་ལ་ཁྲོ་མོའི་རྒྱལ་མོ[P4]་རྣམས་དགོད་དེ*། དེའི་ལག་པ་གཡས་པ་ལ་རོ་ལངས་མའོ། །ལག་པ་གཡོན་པ་ལ་གཞན[D3]་གྱིས་མི་ཐུབ་མའོ། །ཁར་ནི་ཁྲོ་གཉེར་མའོ། །གསང་བར་རལ་གཅིག་མའོ། །ཡང་གཡས་ཀྱི་ཆ་ལ་སྣ་ཚོགས་རྡོ་རྗེ་མའོ། །གཡོན་གྱི[P5]་ཆ་ལ་སྣ་ཚོགས་རིན་ཆེན་མའོ། །པུས་མོ་གཡས་པར་སྣ་ཚོགས་པདྨོའོ། །པུས་མོ་གཡོན་པར་སྣ་ཚོགས་ལས་མའོ། །སྤྱི་བོར་ནམ[D4]་མཁའི་རྡོ་རྗེ་མའོ། །ཁང་པ་གཉིས་ལ་ས་འཛིན་གྱི་ལྷ་མོ་དགོད་པར་བྱའོ་ཞེས་གསུངས་པ[P6]་འདིའི་མདོ་ནི་ལེའུ་བརྒྱད་པ་ལས།

ནུ་མ་གཉིས་ཀྱི་བར་དང་ཧེ་སྲིད་སྤྱི་བོར་ཕྱིན་གྱི*་བར། །
ཁང་པར་ཐུག་གི་བར་དུ་ཡང་ནི་ཆོ་ག་ཤེས་པས་དགོད། །
ཁེད་པ་ལྟེ[N1]་བར་གསང་བའི་རྒྱལ་བའི[D5]་སྲས། ། N174a

3 ba D : bas NPS 5 bstan em. : brtan DNPS 7 gyis NPS : gyi D
8 gyis em. : gyi DNPS 9 de DNP : do S 16 gyi D : gyis NPS

རིགས་ལྔ་རྣམས་ནི་དགོད་པར་ P7 རབ་ཏུ་བྱ། །

ཞེས་གསུངས་སོ། །

[IV.3] དེ་ལྟར་མངོན་པར་འདུས་བྱས་ནས་ཐ་མལ་པའི་བུད་མེད་ཀྱི་རང་བཞིན་བསལ་ཏེ་རིམ་པ་འདིས་རྡོ་རྗེ་དང་པདྨ་བྱིན་གྱིས་བརླབ་པར་བྱའོ། །ཧཱུྃ་གིས་རང་གི་རྟགས་རྡོ་རྗེ་*རྩེ་ལྔ་པར་བསམས་ནས། P8 དབུས་ཀྱི་ D6 རྩེ་མོ་ལ་ཨོཾ་དགོད་པ་ནི་རྡོ་རྗེ་འདུས་བྱ་བའོ། །དེའི་ཆོས་འབྱུང་*ཨཱཿབསམས་ནས་དེ་ལས་སྐྱེས་པའི་པདྨ་འདབ་མ་བརྒྱད་པ་དམར་པོ་བསམ་པ་ནི་པདྨ་འདུས་བྱས་པའོ། །འདིའི་མདོ་ནི་ལེའུ་བདུན་པ་ལས།

P176a ཡི་གེ་ཧཱུྃ་ P1 དང་ཡི་གེ་ཨོཾ། །
S227b S1 ཡི་གེ་ཕཊ་ཀྱང་རྣམ་བརྟགས་*ཏེ། །
D7 འོད་ཟེར་ལྔ་ནི་རྣམ་འཕྲོ་བའི། །
རྡོ་རྗེ་པདྨ་བསྒོམ་པར་བྱ། །

ཞེས་གསུངས་སོ། །

[IV.4] དེ་ལ་རིན་ཆེན་འབྱུང་ལྡན་གྱི་ང་རྒྱལ་དང་ལྡན་པས་ཕན་ཚུན་རྗེས་སུ་ཆགས་པ་སྔོན་ P2 དུ་འགྲོ་བས་*འཁྱུད་པ་དང་འོ་བྱ་བ་ལ་སོགས་པ་བྱས་ནས་ལེའུ་
D203a དྲུག་པ་ལས་གསུངས་པའི་སྔགས་ཀྱིས་* D1 གཉིས་སུ་མེད་པའི་ང་རྒྱལ་བྱའོ། །དེ་ལ་སྔགས་ནི་འདི་ཡིན་ཏེ། ཨོཾ་སརྦ་ཏཐཱ་ག་ཏ་ཨ་ནུ་རཱ་ག*ཎ་སྭ་བྷཱ་བ་ཨཱཏྨ

---

5 rtse DNS : rtsa P **6** āḥ DS : aḥ NP **10** brtags DNP : rtags S **15** 'khyud DNP : khyud S **16** kyis DS : kyi NP **17** a nu rā ga ṇa D : a nu ra ga NPS

*ཀོ་྅ཧཾ་P3 ཞེས་བྱ་བ་རིན་ཆེན་འབྱུང་ལྡན་གྱི་ང་རྒྱལ་གྱིས་*བྱའོ། །དེ་ནས་ཧཱུྃ་གི་སྒྲུ་བླངས་པས་ལས་ལ་གནས་པར་འགྱུར་རོ། །འཛ*ག་པའི་གནས་སྐབས་སུ་ཕཊ་D2 ཀྱི་ཡི་གེ་བརྗོད་པར་བྱའོ། །དེ་ནས་ལུས་ཀྱི་དཀྱིལ་འཁོར་བའི་ལྷ་རྣམས་མཆོག་ཏུ་P4 དགའ་བ*འི་བདེ་བ་ཉམས་སུ་མྱོང་བས་རྩའི་བུ་ག་ནས་ཐིག་ལེ*འི་གཟུགས་ཀྱི*ས་པདྨའི་དབུས་སུ་འབབ་པའོ། །འདིའི་མདོ་ནི་ལེའུ་དང་པོ་ལས་དེ་བཞིན་གཤེགས་པ་ཐམས་ཅད་ཀྱི་སྐུ་དང་། D3 གསུང་དང་། ཐུགས་རྡོ་རྗེའི་བཙུན་P5 མོའི་བྷ་ག་ལ་བཞུགས*་སོ་ཞེས་གསུངས་སོ། །དེ་ལྟ་བུའི་བྱང་ཆུབ་ཀྱི་སེམས་ཀྱི་གནས་སྐབས་སུ་དོན་ཡོད་གྲུབ་པའི་བྱིན་གྱིས་བརླབས་*ལ་ལྷག་པར་མོས་པ་བྱས་ནས་ལེའུ་དྲུག་པ་ལས་གསུངས་པའི་མཆོད་པའི་རིམ་པས་N1 P6 གཉིས་སུ་མེད་པའི་ང་D4 N174b རྒྱལ་བྱའོ། །དེ་ལ་སྔགས་ནི་འདི་ཡིན་ཏེ། ཨོཾ་སརྦ་ཏཐཱ་ག་ཏ་པཱུ་*ཛཱ་བ་ཛྲ་སྭ་བྷཱ་བ་ཨཱཏྨ་*ཀོ་྅ཧཾ་ཞེས་གསུངས་སོ། །

[IV.5] དེ་བཞིན་གཤེགས་པ་ལྔའི་རྗེས་སུ་ཞུགས་པས་བདག་ཉིད་བྱིན་གྱིས་བརླབས་ནས་ཏིང་P7 ངེ་འཛིན་དང་། དབང་བསྐུར་བ་དང་། མཆོད་པ་མཐར་ཐུག་S1 S228a པའི་D5 རིགས་ཐམས་ཅད་ཀྱི་བདག་ཉིད་ཀྱི་ང་རྒྱལ་བྱས་ནས། གཞན་གྱི་དོན་ཕུན་སུམ་ཚོགས་པའི་དོན་དུ་སྲིད་པ་སྐྱེ་བའི་རིམ་པས་དཀྱིལ་འཁོར་གྱི་འཁོར་ལོ་སྤྲོ་བར་བྱའོ། །P8 དེ་ལ་མི་བསྐྱོད་པའི་ཏིང་ངེ་འཛིན་གྱིས་སེམས་ཅན་རྣམས་ཀྱི་ཞེ་སྡང་གི་ཉོན་མོངས་པ་སྦྱོང་བར་བྱེད་དོ། །D6 དེ་བཞིན་དུ་རྣམ་པར་སྣང་མཛད་ཀྱི་ཏིང་ངེ་འཛིན་གྱིས་གཏི་མུག་རྣམ་པར་སྦྱོང་བར་བྱེད་དོ། །རིན་ཆེན་འབྱུང་ལྡན་གྱི་P1 ཏིང་ P176b ངེ་འཛིན་གྱིས་ང་རྒྱལ་རྣམ་པར་སྦྱོང་ངོ་། །འོད་དཔག་ཏུ་མེད་པའི་ཏིང་ངེ་འཛིན་

---

1 ātma ko D : atma ko NPS ○ gyis DNP : gyi S **2** 'dzag NPS : 'jig D
4 ba'i D : ba'o NPS ○ le'i D : le'u NPS **5** kyis D : kyi NPS **7** bźugs D : źugs NPS **8** brlabs la D : brlab pa la NPS **10** pū dzā em. : pū dza DNPS
11 ātma ko D : atma ko NPS

གྱིས*་འདོད་ཆགས་རྣམ་པར་སྦྱོང་ངོ་། །དོན་ཡོད་གྲུབ་པའི་ཏིང་ངེ་འཛིན་[D7]གྱིས་ཕྲག་དོག་རྣམ་པར་སྦྱོང་བོ། །བཅོམ་ལྡན་འདས་དེ་ཉིད་སྤྱན་[P2]མའི་ཏིང་ངེ་འཛིན་གྱིས་སེམས་ཅན་རྣམས་ཀྱི་ནད་ལ་སོགས་པ་ཞི་བར་བྱེད་པའོ། །མཱ་མ་ཀཱིའི་ཏིང་ངེ་འཛིན་གྱིས་རྒྱས་པར་བྱེད་པའོ། །གོས་དཀར་མོའི་ཏིང་ངེ་འཛིན་གྱིས་སྲུང་བར་D203b བྱེད་དོ། །[D1]སྒྲོལ་མའི་ཏིང་ངེ་འཛིན་[P3]གྱིས*་དབང་དུ་བྱེད་དོ། །བཅོམ་ལྡན་འདས་དེ་ཉིད་གཟུགས་རྡོ་རྗེ་ལ་སོགས་པར་གྱུར་ནས། སེམས་ཅན་རྣམས་ཀྱི་བདེ་བ་དང་ཡིད་བདེ*་བསྐྱེད་པར་བྱེད་དོ། །དེ་བཞིན་དུ་བཅོམ་ལྡན་འདས་དེ་ཉིད་སའི་སྙིང་པོ་ལ་[P4]སོགས་པ་བྱང་ཆུབ་སེམས་དཔའ་[D2]རྣམས་ཀྱིས་ཏིང་ངེ་འཛིན་གྱིས་སེམས་ཅན་རྣམས་ཀྱི་སྐྱེ་མཆེད་རྣམས་དག་པར་བྱེད་དོ། །བཅོམ་ལྡན་འདས་དེ་ཉིད་གཤིན་རྗེ་གཤེད་ལ་སོགས་པའི་ཁྲོ་བོ་རྣམས་ཀྱི་ཏིང་ངེ་འཛིན་[P5]གྱིས་ཕྱོགས་བཅུའི་བགེགས་ཀྱི*་ཚོགས་རྣམས་སྡིགས*་པར་བྱེད་དེ*།

བཅོམ་ལྡན་རྡོ་རྗེ་རྣལ་[D3]འབྱོར་ཀུན། །
S228b རྡོ་[S1]རྗེ་སེམས་དཔའ་དེ་བཞིན་གཤེགས། །
དེ་ཡི་ཉེ་བར་ལོངས་སྤྱོད་ཀུན། །
N175a ཁམས་[N1]གསུམ་དག་[P6]ནི་མ་ལུས་པའོ། །

ཞེས་གསུངས་པའི་ཕྱིར་རོ། །དཀྱིལ་འཁོར་གྱི་རྒྱལ་པོ་མཆོག་ཅེས་བྱ་བའི་ཏིང་ངེ་འཛིན་གཉིས་པའོ།། །།

[V.1] དེ་ལྟར་སུམ་ཅུ་རྩ་གཉིས་ཀྱི་[D4]འཁོར་ལོ་མངོན་པར་སྤྲུལ་ནས་ཕྲ་མོའི་[P7]རྣལ་

1 gyis D : gyi NPS 5 gyis DNP : gyi S 7 yid bde DNS : yid P
11 kyi DNP : kyis S ○ sdigs D : bsdigs NPS ○ de NPS : do D

འཁོར་དང་། ཕྱི་ནང་གི་བདག་ཉིད་ཅན་གྱི་བཟླས་པ་བྱ་སྟེ། ཡང་སྔར་བདག་ཉིད་དེ་བཞིན་ཉིད་དུ་གཞུག་པར་བྱའོ། །དེ་ནས་སྤྱན་མ་ལ་སོགས་པའི་ལྷ་མོ་བཞིས་དཀྱིལ་འཁོར་གྱི*་དབུས་ན་བདེ་བ་ཆེན་པོ་མ་མཐོང་བས་བྲལ་བས་སྐྲོ་P8བའི་D5དབང་གིས་རྡོ་རྗེ་ཐུགས་ཁྱོད་ཅེས་བྱ་བ་ལ་སོགས་པའི་གླུ་རྣམས་ཀྱིས་བདེ་བ་ཆེན་པོ་སད་པར་བྱེད་དོ། །དེ་ལ་གླུ་ནི་འདི་ཡིན་ཏེ།

སེམས་ཅན་ཁམས་ན་གནས་ཀྱི་དབང་ཕྱུག་ཁྱོད*་ནི་རྡོ་རྗེའི་ཐུགས། །
དགའ་བ་ཡིད་འོང་དོན་ཆེན་འདོད་པས་P1བདག་ལ་བསྐྱབ་ཏུ་གསོལ། ། P177a
མགོན་D6པོ་གལ་ཏེ་དེ་རིང་བདག་ནི་གསོན་པར་མཆིས་བཞེད་ན། །
སེམས་ཅན་ཡབ་ཆེན་གཉེན་མཆོག་བདག་ལ་དགྱེས་པར་མཛད་དུ་གསོལ། །

རྡོ་རྗེ་སྐུ་ཁྱོད་བཀའ་ཡི་འཁོར་P2ལོ་སེམས་ཅན་ཀུན་ལ་ཕན། །
སངས་རྒྱས་དོན་དུ་བྱང་ཆུབ་དོན་དམ་རབ་ཏུ་ཕན་པར་གཟིགས། །
མགོན་པོ་D7གལ་ཏེ་དེ་རིང་བདག་ནི་གསོན་པར་མཆིས་བཞེད་ན། །
འདོད་ཆགས་དམ་ཚིགས་ཆགས་པས་བདག་ལ་དགྱེས་པར་མཛད་དུ་P3གསོལ། །

ཁྱོད་ནི་རྡོ་རྗེ་གསུང་སྟེ་སེམས་ཅན་ཀུན་ལ་ཕན་ཞིང་ཐུགས་བརྩེ*་བ། །
འཇིག་རྟེན་དག་གི་དགོས་པའི་དོན་མཛད་པ་ལ་རྟག་ཏུ་S1བརྩོན། ། S229a
D1མགོན་པོ་གལ་ཏེ་དེ་རིང་བདག་ནི་གསོན་པར་མཆིས་བཞེད་ན། ། D204a
སྤྱོད་པ*་དྲི་མེད་P4ཀུན་ཏུ་བཟང་པོ་བདག་ལ་དགྱེས་པར་མཛོད། །

[3] gyi DNP : gyis S [6] khyod ni D : om. NPS [15] brtse D : rje NPS
[18] spyod pa DNS : sbyor ba P

ཁྱོད་ནི་རྡོ་རྗེ་འདོད་པ་དམ་ཚིག་མཆོག་གི་ཕན་དོན་ཆེ། །
ཡང་དག་རྫོགས་སངས་རྒྱས་ཀྱི་གདུང་*མཆོག་མཉམ་པ་རྗེས་བརྩེ་བ། །
མགོན་པོ་གལ་ཏེ་དེ་རིང་བདག་ནི་གསོན་པར་མཆིས་ P5 བཞེད་ན། །
N175b D2 ཡོན་ཏན་རིན་ N1 ཆེན་མང་པོའི་གཏེར་གྱུར་བདག་ལ་དགྱེས་པར་མཛོད། །

[V.2] དེ་ལྟར་ཡང་དག་པའི་ཡོན་ཏན་གྱིས་བསྟོད་ནས་སྔོན་གྱི་སྨོན་ལམ་གྱི་དབང་གིས་བཞེངས་ནས་དེ་བཞིན་གཤེགས་པ་རྣམས་ཀྱིས་*མི་བསྐྱོད་པ་ཞེས་ D3 བྱ་བ་ལ་ P6 སོགས་པའི་བསྟོད་པའི་རྒྱལ་པོ་རྣམས་ཀྱིས་*བསྟོད་དེ། དེ་ལ་བསྟོད་པ་ནི་འདི་ཡིན་ཏེ།

མི་བསྐྱོད་པ་ནི་རྡོ་རྗེ་ཆེ། །
རྡོ་རྗེ་དབྱིངས་ནི་མཁས་ཆེན་པོ། །
རྡོ་རྗེ་མཆོག་གསུམ་དཀྱིལ་འཁོར་གསུམ། །
གསང་བའི་དབྱངས་ལ་ཕྱག་འཚལ་ P7 བསྟོད། །

རྣམ་པར་སྣང་མཛད་དག་པ་ཆེ། །
རྡོ་རྗེ་ཞི་བ་ D4 དགའ་བ་ཆེ། །
རང་བཞིན་གྱིས་*ནི་འོད་གསལ་མཆོག །
སྟོན་པ་རྡོ་རྗེ་ཕྱག་འཚལ་བསྟོད། །

རིན་ཆེན་རྒྱལ་པོ་རབ་ཏུ་ཟབ། །
རྡོ་རྗེ་ནམ་མཁའ་དྲི་མ་མེད། །

2 gduṅ D : mduṅ NPS **6** rnams kyis em. : rnams kyi D; om. NPS
7 kyis D : kyi NPS **15** gyis NPS : gyi D

རང་བཞིན་དག་པ་* P8 གོས་པ་མེད། །
གསང་བའི་དབྱིངས་ལ་ཕྱག་འཚལ་བསྟོད། །

རྡོ་རྗེ་དཔག་མེད་རྒྱལ་པོ་ཆེ། །
D5 མི་རྟོག་ནམ་མཁའ་རྡོ་རྗེ་འཛིན། །
འདོད་ཆགས་ཕ་རོལ་ཕྱིན་པ་བརྙེས། །
རྡོ་རྗེ་གསུང་ལ་ཕྱག་འཚལ་བསྟོད། །

དོན་ཡོད་རྡོ་རྗེ་རྫོགས་P1 སངས་རྒྱས། । P177b
བསམ་པ་ཐམས་ཅད་རྫོགས་མཛད་པ། །
དག་པ་S1 ངོ་བོ་ཉིད་ལས་བྱུང་། । S229b
རྡོ་རྗེ་སེམས་དཔའ་ཕྱག་འཚལ་བསྟོད། །

[V.3] D6 དེའི་རྗེས་ལ་སངས་རྒྱས་ཀྱི་ཡེ་ཤེས་ཡང་དག་པར་གསལ་བར་བྱས་ནས་དཀྱིལ་འཁོར་ལ་རྗེས་P2 སུ་ཆགས་པར་བྱས་ལ་སྔར་བཞིན་དུ་རང་གི་ལུས་ཀྱི་དཀྱིལ་འཁོར་ལ་བཅུག་ནས་རིམ་པ་འདིས་ཉེ་བར་བསྡུ་བར་བྱའོ། །རང་གི་སྙིང་གར་གནས་པའི་ཧཱུྃ་བརྗོད་ནས་དེས་སེམས་ཅན་གྱི་D7 ཁམས་ཐམས་ཅད་རྡོ་རྗེ་འཆང་ཆེན་པོའི་P3 གཟུགས་ཀྱིས་ཡོངས་སུ་གྱུར་པར་བསམས་*ནསདེ་ཡིད་ལ་བྱེད་པར་གནས་པར་བྱའོ། །འདིའི་མདོ་ནི་ལེའུ་བཅུ་གཉིས་པ་ལས།

ནམ་མཁའི་ཁམས་ཀྱི་དབུས་གནས་པར། །
བཀོད་པའི་དཀྱིལ་འཁོར་བསྒོམ་པར་བྱ། །

---

1 pa NPS : pas D   15 yoṅs su gyur par bsams nas D : yoṅs su gyur pa'i gzugs nas NPS

D204b ཧཱུྃ་ནི་དེ་ཡི་དབུས་གནས་པར། །
རང་གི་གཟུགས་བརྙན་རབ་ཏུ་བརྟག །

ཅེས་གསུངས་སོ། །

[V.4] དེ་ལྟར་ལས་དང་པོ་པའི་དམ་ཚིག་དང་སྡོམ་པ་ལ་གནས་ཤིང་དབང་ཐོབ་པས་ཐ་མལ་པའི་ང་རྒྱལ་བསལ་ལ་ཐུན་བཞིར་ལྷའི་རྣལ་འབྱོར་གོམས་པར་བྱེད་པས་བདག་དང་གཞན་གྱི་དོན་ཕུན་སུམ་ཚོགས་པ་ལ་མོས་པས་ཞི་བའི་ལས་ལ་སོགས་པ་ཤིན་ཏུ་ཁྱད་པར་ཅན་ཡང་བྱའོ། །སྒྲུབ་ཐབས་ལས་གསུངས་པའི་རིམ་པས་ཁ་ཟས་སྦྱང་བ་དང་། སྙིང་ག་སྦྱང་བ་དང་། ལྐོག་མ་སྦྱང་བ་དང་། ཁ་ཟས་ཀྱི་བྱ་བ་བྱས་ནས་བདེ་བར་འཛུག་པར་འགྱུར་རོ། །ཕྱི་དང་ནང་གི་བདག་ཉིད་ཅན་གྱི་སྦྱིན་སྲེག་ཡི་གེ་གསུམ་མམ། ཕྲེང་བའི་སྔགས་སམ། སྔགས་དང་སྨན་གྱི་སྦྱོར་བས་ཀྱང་རྡོ་རྗེ་དང་པདྨ་མཉམ་པར་སྦྱར་བ་བྱས་ནས་ལས་ཐམས་ཅད་བསྒྲུབ་པར་བྱའོ། །ཞེས་བྱ་བ་ནི་ལས་ཀྱི་རྒྱལ་པོ་མཆོག་ཅེས་བྱ་བའི་ཏིང་ངེ་འཛིན་གསུམ་པའོ།། །།

(N176a, S230a)

[Colophon] དཔལ་གསང་བ་འདུས་པ་རྣལ་འབྱོར་ཆེན་པོའི་རྒྱུད་ཀྱི་སྙིད་པ་སྐྱེ་བའི་རིམ་པས་རྡོ་རྗེ་སེམས་དཔའི་སྒྲུབ་ཐབས་སློབ་དཔོན་ཟླ་བ་གྲགས་པས་མཛད་པ་རྫོགས་སོ།། །།

གཞུང་འདིའི་ཚད་ནི་ཀང་པ་དང་བཅས་པའི་བརྒྱ་ཕྲག་གཉིས་པའོ།། །།

P178a དཔལ་བི་ཀྲ་མ་ཤཱི་ལའི་གཙུག་ལག་ཁང་ཆེན་པོར་པཎྜི་ཏ་མཁས་པ་ཆེན་པོ་ཏ་ཐཱ་

[2] rab em.; dag D : rtag NPS [5] bsal D : gsal NPS [6] gyi DNP : gyis S [10] gyi D : gyis NPS [15] ba D : ba'i NPS [16] so DN : s+ho PS [18] dpal bi kra ma D : dpal+bi kra ma la NPS

ག་ཏ་ར་ཀླིཏའི་ཞལ་སྔ་ནས་དང་། ལོ་ཙྪ་བ་ཀློག་*སྐྱ་གཞོན་ནུ་འབར་གྱིས་བསྒྱུར་རོ།། །།

སླད་ཀྱིས་དཔལ་ཐོ་*ལིང་དཔེ་མེད་ལྷུན་གྱིས་གྲུབ་པའི་གཙུག་ལག་ཁང་དུ་རྒྱ་P2གར་གྱི་མཁན་པོ་མཁས་པ་ཆེན་པོ་དཱི་པཾ་ཀ་ར་རཀྵི་ཏ་དང་། ཁམས་པ་D6དགེ་སློང་ལོ་ཙྪ་བ་བ་རིས་བཙོས་ཤིང་བཤད་དེ་ཞུས་ནས་གཏན་ལ་ཕབ་*པའོ།། །།

1 klog skya em. : bklog skya D; glog kya NPS 3 tho liṅ D : om. NPS
5 pa'o D : pa NPS

Appendices

Appendix 1: Quotations from the *Vajrasattvaniṣpādanasūtra* in an Anonymous Text (VNU*)

1 (VNU* 5b3–6a1/VS II.1): तत्र तावत्साधनक्रमः प्रदर्श्यते ।

मन्त्रावधारणं पूर्वं द्वितीयं न्यासदेशना ।
व्यवस्थो*लिस्तृतीया तु चतुर्थं तत्त्वदर्शनम् ॥

इत्यनुक्रमेण साधनोपयिकां श्रुत्वा वज्रगुरोराज्ञां प्राप्य साधको महाटव्यादिमनोऽ*नुकूलप्रदेशे पूर्वाभिमुखः सत्त्वपर्यङ्केनोपविश्य सर्वसत्त्वेषु महाकरुणाचित्तमुत्पा*द्य स्वपरहितहेतोर्वक्ष्यमाणक्रमेण वज्रसत्त्व*रूपं साधयेत् ॥

2 (VNU* 7b3–5/VS II.2): तदनन्तरं साधकः शून्यताधिमोक्षेण प्राकृताहङ्कारमपनीय झटित्यात्मानं महावज्रधररूपं शुक्लवर्णं द्विभुजमेकवक्त्रं विश्वपद्मचन्द्रासनासीनं प्रभामण्डलविराजितं द्वात्रिंशन्महालक्ष*णधरं व्यञ्जनाशीतिभूषितं वज्रधात्वीश्वर्यालिङ्गितमायोपमदेहं

---

7 vyavastholi<s> em. : vyavastholi Ms **9** °mano'nukūla° em. : °manokūle Ms **10** utpādya em. : utpāda'dya Ms ○ vajrasattvarūpaṃ em. : vajrasatva¨¨ṃ Ms **15** °lakṣa{dha}ṇadharaṃ Ms

ध्यायात् ॥

3 (VNU* 7b5–8a3/VS II. 3): ततो ज्ञानप्रदीपवज्रसमाधिन्यायेन वज्रधृगिति मन्त्रमुच्चार्य तेनाक्षोभ्यरूपं कृष्णवर्णं त्रिमुखं षड्भुजं आत्मपुरःस्थं दृष्ट्वा पुनस्तं स्वकाये क्षीरोदकन्यायेनानुप्रवेश्येन्द्रनीलवर्णमात्मानमीषद्दंष्ट्रोत्कटभीषणं पतितुल्याकृतिस्पर्शवज्रालिङ्गितमायोपमदेहं सूर्यासनं दक्षिणे वज्रचक्रपद्मधरं वामे घण्टाचिन्तामणिखड्गान्वितं द्वेषवज्ररूपं त्रिसत्त्वात्मकं विचिन्तयेत् ॥

4 (VNU* 8a3–4/VS II.4.1): एवं द्वेषवज्रसमाधिस्थो मन्त्री दीर्घहूंकारमुच्चार्य तज्जनितयमान्तकादिदशक्रोधान् त्रिमुखषड्भुजान् वक्ष्यमाणनानाप्रहरणव्यग्रहस्तान् दुष्टतर्जनतत्परान् दशदिग्मण्डलाग्रे विचिन्तयेत् ॥

5 (VNU* 8a4–b1/VS II.4.2): ततो निसुम्भराजमधस्ताद्द्वितीयं निसुम्भराजं निर्मायागत्य स्वपुरःस्थं किङ्कररूपेणाज्ञां मार्गयन्तं वि-

4 °pura<ḥ>sthaṃ em. : °purasthaṃ Ms ○ dr(ṣṭvā) Ms ○ puna(s taṃ sva)kāye Ms 5 °(nyā)yenā(nu)praveśya Ms ○ ā(tmā)naṃ Ms ○ (ī)ṣad° Ms ○ °otka(ṭa)bhī(ṣa)ṇaṃ Ms 6 °sparśa(vajrāliṅgi)ta° Ms ○ °(de)haṃ Ms ○ da(kṣi)ṇe Ms 7 (ghaṇṭā)° Ms ○ °ā(nvita)ṃ Ms ○ trisa(tvātmakaṃ) Ms 9 °samādhi(stho) Ms ○ m{o}antrī Ms 10 ta(jja)nita° Ms ○ °yamāntakādi em. : °jamāntakādi Ms ○ (daśa)krodhān⁰ Ms ○ °bhu(jān⁰) Ms 11 (vakṣya)māṇa° Ms ○ daśadi(gmaṇḍa)lāgre Ms 13 (ta)to Ms ○ adha(stāt*) Ms 14 nirmāyāgatya em. : nirmmāya'gatya Ms ○ svapura<ḥ>sthaṃ em. : svapurasthaṃ Ms

चिन्त्य चतुर्हूंकारमन्त्रेणाज्ञां दद्यात् । तत्रायं मन्त्रः — ओं सुम्भ निसुम्भ हूं गृह्ण २ हूं गृह्णापय गृह्णापय हूं आनय होः भगवन् विद्याराज हूं फट् ॥

6 (VNU* 8b1–2/VS II.4.3): ततो निसुम्भराजं दशदिशो गत्वा इन्द्रादिविघ्नाधिपतीनङ्कुशेन हृदि विद्धाकृष्य पाशेन गलके बद्धा दशक्रोधानां प्रतिपादयन्तं विचिन्तयेत् ॥

7 (VNU* 9b3–10a2/VS II.4.3): ततो ऽमृतकुण्डलिरुत्तरद्वारे द्वितीयनिर्माणं संस्थाप्यात्मानं दशकीलकाकारं वज्रामृतमहाराजं नीलोत्पलदलश्यामं ज्वालामालाकुलप्रभं नाभिदेशादधोभागं शूलाकारं ऊर्ध्वं क्रोधाकृतिं त्रिमुखाकारषड्भुजं दशविघ्नाधिपतीनां शिरसि निपतितं पादतलं यावद्विचिन्तयेत् । ततो निसुम्भराजं व्युत्थाय यमान्तकदत्तनिर्मितवज्रमुद्गरेण मन्त्रमावर्त्य कोटयन्तं ध्यायात् । तत्रायं मन्त्रः — ओं घ घ घ घ घातय घातय सर्वदुष्टान् फट् फट् कीलय कीलय सर्वपापान् फट् फट् हूं हूं वज्रकील वज्रधरो आज्ञापयति सर्वविघ्नानां कायवाक्चित्तवज्रं कीलय हूं हूं फट् फट् ॥

8 (VNU* 10a3–5/VS II.4.4): ततष्टक्किराजमन्त्रेण लोहजलाग्नि-

1 ca(tu)r° Ms ○ °ā(jñāṃ da)dyāt* Ms **8** saṃsthā{pa}pya Ms
11 nisu<mbha>rājaṃ em. : nisurājaṃ Ms **13** ghātaya em. : ghātaka Ms
14 (pha)ṭ⁰ Ms **15** °vajra<ṃ> em. : °vajra Ms **16** tataḥ ṭa(kki)rāja° Ms

वायुप्राकारचतुष्टयं यथाक्रमं चतुरस्रादिभेदेन बाह्यतो विचिन्तयेत् । तत्रायं मन्त्रः — नमः समन्तकायवाक्चि*त्तवज्राणां टक्कि हूं जः । ततो भ्रूंकारेण वज्रपञ्जरं विचिन्त्य लो*हप्राकालोपरि व्यवस्थितम्' त्र्यक्षरेण कवचादिकम्' हूंकारेण विश्ववज्रमय*ं भूभा*गं विचिन्तयेत् ॥

9 (VNU* 10b2–4/VS II.4.6): एवं कृते ऽपि विघ्नोपशम*ने रक्षाचक्रं त्रैधातुकं च तथतायां प्रवेशयेद्बोधिचित्तगाथया । तत्रेयं गाथा —

अभावे भावनाभावो भावना नैव भावना ।
इति भावो न भाव*ः स्याद्भावना नोपलभ्यते ॥

इति । इयमपि परमा रक्षा ॥

10 (VNU* 10b4–11a1/VS II.5.1): तत्राकाशधातुमध्ये यंकारजवायुमण्डलं कोदण्डाकृतिं हूंकारद्वयेन पार्श्वयोर्वज्रद्वयाङ्कितं विचिन्त्य तदुपरि रंकारेण त्रिकोणाग्निमण्डलं तथा वज्रद्वयान्वितम्' पुनस्तदुपरि वंकारेण वर्तुलं वारुणमण्डलं तथा वज्रद्वयाङ्कितं' तदुपरि लंकारेण चतुर*स्रं माहेन्द्रमण्डलं तथा वज्रद्वयाङ्कितं विभाव्य मण्डलचतुष्टयं संह*त्य विश्ववज्रमयं भूभागं ध्यायात् ॥

---

2 °(ci)tta° Ms **3** loha° em. : jo¦ha° Ms **4** °maya(ṃ) Ms ○ bhūbhāga<ṃ> em. : bhūbhāga Ms **5** °opaśamane em. : °opasa¦mane Ms **9** bhāva(ḥ) Ms **15** catu‹ra›sraṃ Ms **16** saṃhṛtya em. : saṃ(skṛ)tya Ms

11 (VNU* 11a1–3/VS II.5.2): एवमाधारमण्डलं निष्पाद्य भ्रूं-कारेण कूटागारम्

चतुरस्रं चतुर्द्वारं चतुस्तोरणशोभितम् ।
चतुःसूत्रसमायुक्तमष्टस्तम्भोपशोभितम् ॥

हारार्धहाररचितं मणिवज्रार्धचन्द्रकम्* ।
खचितं वज्ररत्नैस्तु द्वारनिर्यू*हसन्धिषु ॥

कुम्भस्तम्भमहावज्रं क्र*यशीर्षश्च पक्षिणी ।
घण्टापताका*संशो*भं चामरादिविभूषितम् ॥

इति ।

12 (VNU* 11a3–b1/VS III.1.1): एवङ्गुणविशिष्टं देवमनुष्यातिक्रान्तं प्रासादवरं वज्रभूभागोपरि विचिन्त्य विश्वपद्मोपरि चन्द्राद्यासनं संस्थाप्य झटिति महावज्रधररूपमात्मानमिन्द्रनीलवर्णं त्रिमुखषड्भुजं दक्षिणे वज्रचक्रपद्मधरं वामे घण्टाचिन्तामणिखड्गान्वितं सम्पुटयोगेन मध्यमण्डले पद्मचन्द्रास*ने सत्त्वपर्यङ्केणोपविष्टं विचिन्तयेत् ॥

5 maṇivajrārdhacandrakam em. : maṇicandrārddhavajrakaṃ Ms **6** °ni(ryūha)° Ms. **7** kraya° em. : krama° Ms **8** °patākā° em. : °pa(trā)kā° Ms ○ °saṃ(śo)bhaṃ Ms **14** (padmacandrā)sane Ms

13 (VNU* 12b5–13a4/VS III.1.5): एवं प्रभास्वरालम्बनेन सकलक्लेशमलं प्रक्षाल्य तस्मादात्मानं वज्रसत्त्वं महामुद्रारूपं निष्पादयेदनेन क्रमेण। प्रभास्वरात् हूंकारेण सूर्यमण्डलम्' तदुपरि ओंकारेण चन्द्रमण्डलम्' पुनस्तदुपरि आःकारेण र*क्ताष्टदलपद्मम्' पद्मोपरि ओं आः हूं इत्यक्षरत्रयमुपर्युपरि विन्यस्य* सर्वं सूर्यादिकं संहृत्य परिपूर्णचन्द्रमण्डलाकारपरिणतं चित्तमात्रं विचिन्तयेत् । तद्रश्मिनिवहैर्जगत्स्थावरजङ्गममानीय तत्रैवान्तर्भाव्य ओं धर्मधातुस्वभावात्मको ऽहमिति मन्त्रेण स्वचित्तरत्नं दृढीकुर्यादिति प्रथमो योगः ॥

14 (VNU* 13a5–b2/VS III.2): ततश्चन्द्रमण्डलोपरि त्र्यक्षरं तेन पञ्चसूचि*कं महाव*ज्रं वज्रचन्द्रपरिणतं महावज्रध*ररूपं द्विभुजमेकवक्त्रं शुक्लवर्णं ज्ञानमयदेहं ध्यायादि*ति। एवं वैरोचना*दियोगी शान्तिकादिकर्माणि तथैव सूर्यादिपरिणतं पूर्णचन्द्रमण्डलम्' तदुपरि त्र्यक्ष*रपरिणतचक्रादिना तथैव म*हावज्रधररूपं भावयेदित्याम्नायः। द्वितीयो ऽनुयोगः ॥

15 (VNU* 13b2–4/VS III.3.1): एवं योगानुयोगे क्रमेणात्मानं सम्भोगकायं निष्पाद्य चरमभविकवत्सत्त्वार्थं* प्रति ओंका-

4 ra(ktā)° Ms **5** v{ā}inyasya Ms **11** °sūcikaṃ em. : °śūcikaṃ Ms ○ °vajra<ṃ> em. : °vajra Ms ○ mahāvajradha<ra>° em. : mahāvajradha° Ms **12** (dhyāyād i)ti Ms ○ vairocanādi em. : vau¦rocanādi° Ms **14** tryakṣara{ṃ}° Ms ○ ma¨hā° Ms **17** caramabhavika(vat satvārthaṃ) Ms

रादिबीजजनितवैरोचना*दिस्वभावस्कन्धधात्वायतनानुप्रवेशेन निर्माणकायमात्मानं निष्पादयेत् । शिरःस्थानादिकं प्रभास्वरं ध्यात्वा तत्रैव वैरोचना*दिदेवताबीजं न्यसेदनेन क्रमेण । तत्रायं क्रमः —

[a]वैरोचनीयबीजं *तु ओंकारं शुक्लवर्णकम् ।
रूपस्कन्धस्वभावेन न्यसे*न्मूर्धनि मन्त्रवित् ॥

आःकारममिताभस्य सञ्ज्ञास्कन्धस्वभावकम् ।
रक्तवर्णं मुखे ध्यात्वा वागैश्वर्यमवाप्नुयात् ॥

अक्षोभ्यस्य तु हूंकारं राजावर्तकसुप्रभम् ।
न्यसेद्धृदये मन्त्री विज्ञानस्कन्धरूपतः ॥

स्वाकारं रत्ननाथस्य वेदनास्कन्धरूप*तः ।
पीतवर्णं न्यसेन्नाभौ वेदनाशु*द्धिहेतुकम् ॥

पादद्वये तु हाकारं संस्कारस्कन्धभावतः ।[a]

16 (VNU* 15a1–2/VS III.4.1): एवं योगानुयोगाभ्या*मतियोगक्रमेण च श्रीवज्रसत्त्वरूपं निश्चित्य कायमण्डलसम्पन्नो योगी पुनर्घटमाननिष्पन्नदेवताविकल्पापनयार्थं चतुर्थं महायोगं कुर्यात् ॥

---

[a] Pi 55–58ab (not in VS)

---

1 °vairocanādi° em. : °vau¦rocanādi° Ms **3** vairocanādi° em. : vo¦rocanādi Ms **4** vairocanīyabijaṃ tu em. : vau¦rocanīyabīj(ant)u Ms **5** nyasen em. : nyasye¦n Ms **10** °rūpataḥ em. : °rūpat*¦ Ms **11** °śuddhi° em. : °su¦ddhi° Ms **13** yogānuyogābhyām em. : yogānuyogābhyāṃ¦m Ms

17 (VNU* 15a5–b5/VS III.4.1):

प्रार्थयेत्तु* ततो मन्त्री गाथाद्वयम् उदाहरन् ॥

बुद्धकायधरः श्रीमांस्त्रि*वज्राभेद्यभावितः ।
अधिष्ठानपदं मे ऽद्य करोतु कायवज्रिणः ॥

दशदिक्संस्थिता बुद्धास्त्रिवज्राभेद्यभाविताः ।
अधिष्ठानपदं मे ऽद्य* कुर्वन्तु कायवज्रिणः ॥

अध्येषणानन्तरं देवताव्यूह*मन्यो*न्यानुरागणपूर्वकं परमानन्दसुखमनुभूय श्वे*तरश्मिस्वभावे*न ज्ञानसत्त्व*वद्वै*रोचनद्वारेण प्रविश्य ज्ञानभूमिं प्राप्य समस्तकाय*मापूर्य प्रीणयन्तं विचिन्त्य दृढीकुर्यादनया गाथया* —

यत्कायं सर्वबुद्धानां पञ्चस्कन्धप्रपूरितम् ।
बुद्धकायस्वभावेन ममापि तादृशं भवेत् ॥

इति । अत्रानेनै*व मन्त्रेणाद्वयाहङ्कारं कुर्या*त् — ओं सर्वतथागतकायवज्रस्वभावात्मको ऽहम् ॥

18 (VNU* 15b5–16a5/VS III.4.2): वाक्चित्तयोरप्यने*न क्र-

---

2 prārthayet <tu> em. (Pi 72c) : prārthayet Ms **3** buddhakā(yadharaḥ śrī)mān⁰ Ms **6** °(padaṃ me ')dya Ms **7** °(vyūha)m Ms ○ a(nyonyā)° Ms **8** (śve)ta° Ms ○ °(sva)bhāvena Ms ○ jñāna(satvava)t* Ms ○ vairocana° em. : vau'rocana° Ms **9** °kā(ya)m Ms ○ a(nayā) gā(thayā) Ms **13** atrā(nenai)va Ms ○ °āhaṅkā(raṃ kuryāt*) Ms **15** a(py anena) Ms

मेणाधिष्ठा*नं कुर्यात् । तत्रायं क्रमः — आःकारं रक्तवर्णं जिह्वापद्मोपरि विन्यस्य तज्जनितपाण्डरवासिनीव्यूहैर्गगनमापूर्य पूर्ववदमिताभव्यूहं दृष्ट्वा अध्येषयेदनया गाथया —

धर्मौ* वै वाक्पथ*ः श्रीमांस्त्रिवज्राभेद्यभावितः ।
अधिष्ठानपदं मे ऽद्य करोतु वाग्वज्रिणः ॥

दशदिक्संस्थिता बुद्धास्त्रिवज्राभेद्यभाविताः ।
अधिष्ठानपदं मे ऽद्य कुर्वन्तु वाग्वज्रिणः ॥

एवमध्येषिते पूर्ववद्वीन्द्रियसमापत्त्या महारागानलेन व्यूहद्वयं द्रवीभूय रक्तरश्मिरूपेण मुखे प्रवेश्याशेषवागैश्वर्यमासादयन्तं विचिन्त्य दृढीकुर्यादनया गाथया —

यदेव वज्रधर्मस्य वाचा निरुक्तिसम्पदः ।
ममापि तादृशी वाचा भवेद्धर्मधरोपमा* ॥

इति । ततो ऽनेन मन्त्रेणाद्वयाहङ्कारं कुर्यात् — ओं सर्वतथागतवाग्वज्रस्वभावात्मको* ऽहमिति ॥

19 (VNU* 16b1–6/VS III.4.3): ततः स्वहृ*दि चन्द्रस्थवज्रवरटके* कृष्णहूं*कारं विचिन्त्य तज्जनितमामकीव्यूहं गगनकुहरे* वि-

---

1 (krameṇā)dhiṣṭhānaṃ Ms **4** vai em. : vau! Ms ○ vākpatha‹ḥ› Ms **12** °opamā em. : °opama Ms **14** °svabhā<vā>tmako em. : °svabhātmako Ms **15** (tataḥ svahṛ)di Ms **16** ca(ndrastha)vajravara‹ṭa›ke Ms ○ (kṛṣṇa)hūṃkāra(ṃ) Ms ○ gagana(kuhare) Ms

चिन्त्य पूर्ववज्झटित्यक्षोभ्यव्यूहं चान्तरीक्षे दृष्ट्वा प्रार्थयेदनया गाथया —

वज्रचित्तधरः श्रीमांस्त्रिवज्राभेद्यभावितः ।
अधिष्ठानपदं मे ऽद्य करोतु चित्तवज्रिणः ॥

दशदिक्संस्थि*ता बुद्धास्त्रिवज्राभेद्यभाविताः ।
अधिष्ठानपदं मे ऽद्य कुर्वन्तु चित्तवज्रिणः ॥

प्रार्थनानन्तरं पूर्ववद्व्यूहद्वयं महारागानले*न द्रवीभूय कृष्णरश्मिरूपेण हृदये प्रविश्य चित्तैश्वर्यमासादयन्तं* विचिन्त्य दृढीकुर्यादनया गाथया —

यच्चित्तं समन्तभद्र*स्य गुह्यकेन्द्रस्य धीमत*ः ।
ममापि तादृशं चित्तं भवेद्वज्रधरोपमम्* ॥

इति । ततो ऽनेनाद्वयाहङ्कारं कुर्यात् — ओं सर्वतथागतचित्तवज्रस्वभावात्मको ऽहम् इति ॥

20 (VNU* 16b6–17a1/VS III.4.4): एवं कुलत्रयप्रवेशे*न कायवाक्चि*त्तं पृथगधिष्ठाय पुनस्त्रिव*ज्राभेद्यस्वभावं महावज्राधिष्ठानं कु-

5 (daśadiksaṃ)sthitā Ms **7** mahā(rāgānalena) Ms **8** (āsāda)yantaṃ Ms
10 (samanta)bhadrasya Ms ○ (dhī)mataḥ Ms **11** °opama(ṃ) Ms
14 °(praveśena) Ms **15** kā(yavā)kcittaṃ Ms ○ pu(nas tri){va}
++++++++++ vajrā° Ms

र्यादनेन मन्त्रेण — ओं सर्वतथागतकायवाक्चित्तवज्रस्वभावात्मको ऽहमिति ॥

21 (VNU* 17a2–4/VS III.4.5): एवं समयसत्त्वं निष्पाद्य तस्य हृदये ज्ञानसत्त्वं द्विभुजं रक्तवर्णं सम्पुटयोगेन विचिन्त्य स्वमुकुटे ऽधिपतिं शुक्लवर्णं द्विभुजं सम्पुटयोगेन स्फरद्बोधिचित्तधारया सर्वशरीरं प्रीणयन्तं ध्यायात्* ॥

22 (VNU* 17a4–5/VS III.4.5): एवं समयसत्त्वहृदये ज्ञानसत्त्वं विचिन्त्य तस्यापि हृदये हूंकारं समाधिसत्त्वाख्यं चतुर्षु पार्श्वेषु ओंकारादिपरिवेष्टितं सततोदयं* बृहत्प्रदीपसदृशमज्ञानान्धकारविधूननार्थमालोकपुञ्जाकारं ध्यायात् ॥

23 (VNU* 17b1–18b3/VS IV.1): एवं योगचतुष्टयेन त्रिसत्वात्मतयात्मानं स्वार्थसम्पत्स्वभावं समाधिराजाग्रीमुत्पाद्येदानीं* परार्थसम्पत्तये मण्डलराजाग्रीसमाधिप्रदर्शनाय* पीठिकावतार्यते* — वैरोचनादिभावकः* ओंकारादिसमाधिसत्त्वं भावयेत् । भगवाञ्शाक्यमुनिः सर्वं* कृत्वा तुषितवर*भुवनादवतीर्य वीतरागरूपमभिनिर्माय* श्रावकगोत्राञ्श्रावकमार्गे प्रतिष्ठाप्य पुनर्महाया-

---

6 dhyāyat em. : dhyāyet*¦ Ms **9** satatodayaṃ em. : satatodva¦yaṃ Ms **12** samādhirā(jā)grī(m utpādya) Ms **13** °pradarśanā(ya) Ms ∘ pīṭhikā° em. : pīṭhī¦kā° Ms **14** vairocanādibhāvakaḥ em. : vau¦rocanādibhāvaka(ḥ) Ms **15** (sarvaṃ) Ms ∘ tuṣita(vara)° Ms **16** °rū(pam a)bhinirmmāya Ms

निकबोधिसत्त्वानां स्कन्धविज्ञानकायादिधर्मनैरात्म्याधिगमं भूमिपारमितामार्गं चर्यां च सम्प्रकाश्य गम्भीराधिमुक्तिकानां सत्यद्वयाधिगमा*द्रागबोधिप्रदर्शनार्थमेतत् । श्रीसमाजपटलोक्तमहारागनयं नाम समाधिं समापन्नः । तथा घटमानयोगिनाप्यादियोगं कृत्वा रागचरितसत्त्वानां काममोक्षप्रदर्शनाय सप्तदशपटलोक्तसर्वकामोपभोगसमाधिना विहर्तव्यमनेन क्रमेण । तत्रायं क्रमः —

प्राप्य कन्यां विशालाक्षीं रूपयौवनमण्डिताम् ।
नीलोत्पलदलश्यामां रजकस्य महात्मनः ॥

सुशिक्षितां समादाय साधके भक्तिवत्सलाम् ।
पुरतो ऽवस्थाप्य तां कुर्यात्पञ्चकुलकलापिनीम् ॥

ततो वज्रपद्मसंस्कारपूर्वकां* द्वीन्द्रियसमापत्तिं कृत्वा बोधिचित्तादक्षोभ्यादिमण्डलचक्रमभिनिर्माय तत्तत्समाधिना सत्त्वानां द्वेषादिक्लेशान्विशोध्य पुनरानी*य समाधिनाक्षोभ्या*दीन्स्वकायमण्डले प्रवेशयेत् । अन्यां*श्च स्वकस्वकेष्वासनेषु निषण्णान्विचिन्तयेत् । अथ वा स्वहृ*दयाज्ज्ञानमुद्रामभिनिर्माय तया सह समापत्तिं कृत्वा मन्त्रैकनिर्माणैः सत्त्वार्थं कुर्यात्'

हृदयस्था महादेवी योगिनां योगवाहिनी ।
जननी सर्वबुद्धानां वज्रधात्वीश्वरी स्मृता ॥

---

3 °ādhigamā(t^0) Ms **11** °pūrvakāṃ em. : °pūrvvakaṃ Ms **13** ānīya ···· Ms ◦ ····(samādhinā'kṣobhyā)dīn^0 Ms (2 akṣaras illegible) **14** a(nyāṃ)ś ca Ms. **15** svahṛ‹da›yāt* Ms

इति वचनात् ॥

24 (VNU* 18b3–19a1/VS IV.2): एवं बाह्याध्यात्मिकमुद्रां निश्चित्येदानीं पञ्चकुलकलापिनीक्रमः प्रदर्श्यते। ओंकारं शिरसि' आःकारं मुखे' हूंकारं हृदये' स्वा नाभौ' हा द्विपादयोर्न्यसेत् । चतुर्भूतस्वभावेन लोचनां मामकीं पाण्डरवासिनीं तारां च न्यसेत् । रूपादिविषयेषु रूपवज्रां शब्दवज्रां गन्धवज्रां रसवज्रां स्पर्शवज्रां च। चक्षुराद्यायतनेषु क्षितिगर्भादीनां थ्लीं-ओं-ओं-ओं-हूं-ओं-मैं-सं-बीजानि न्यसेत् । पुनस्तस्या भुजाद्यवयवे क्रोधराज्ञीं न्यसेत् ॥

25 (VNU* 19b1–5/VS IV.4): रत्नसम्भवाहङ्कारवान्योग्यन्योन्यानुरागणपूर्वकमालिङ्गनचुम्बनादिकं कृत्वाद्वयाहङ्कारं कुर्यादनेन मन्त्रेण — ओं सर्वतथागतानुरागणवज्रस्वभावात्मको ऽहमिति। हूंकारगीतिमुच्चारयन्योषित्कर्मस्थो भवेत् । स्फरणावस्थायां फट्कारमुच्चारयेत् । ततः कायमण्डलदेवताः परमानन्दसुखमनुभूय नाडीविवराद्बिन्दुरूपेण पद्ममध्ये निपतिता विचिन्तयेत् । एवं बोधिचित्तोत्सर्गावस्थायाममोघसिद्ध्यधिष्ठानमधिमुच्य दशदिक्संस्थितान्बुद्धान्पूजयेद्गरुडमुद्रयानेन मन्त्रेण — ओं सर्वतथागतपूजावज्रस्वभावात्मको ऽहम् ॥

3 (oṃ)kāraṃ Ms **9** (ratna)sambhavā° Ms **10** °pūrvakam em. : °pūrvakaṃ!m Ms **12** u(ccāraya)n^{0} Ms **13** °maṇḍa<la>° em. : °maṇḍa° Ms

26 (VNU* 19b5–20a1/VS IV.5): एवं पञ्चतथागतानुप्रवेशेनात्मानमधिष्ठाय समाध्यभिषेकपूजापर्यन्तं सर्वकर्मकारतरं कृत्वा परार्थसम्पत्तये भवोत्पत्तिक्रमेण मण्डलचक्रमुत्सृजेत् ॥

Appendix 2:
An Edition of the *Mantroddhāra*

नमो बुद्धाय ॥

G2 श्रीगुह्यसमाजमहायोगतन्त्रस्य साधनोपायिकानुपूर्वीं G3 दर्शयन्नाह —

*मन्त्रावधारणं पूर्वं द्वीतीया न्यासदेशना ।
*व्यवस्थोलिस्तृतीया च चतुर्थं तत्त्वदर्शनम् ॥

इति। अस्य सूत्रस्यायमर्थः — प्रथमं तावदशेषमन्त्रपदं साधनाङ्गादुद्धृत्य चेतस्येवावरोप्यावधारयेदिति G4 *मन्त्रावधारणं पूर्वम् । ततः स्कन्धधात्वायतनादिषु वैरोचनाद्याकारेण स्वकायमण्डले न्यसेदिति द्वितीया न्यासदेशना। विन्यस्तदेवतानामेकैकस्यानुपूर्वेण स्वलक्षणं परिज्ञाय G5 *निरूपितं देवताचक्रमिति व्यवस्थोलिस्तृतीया। *सूक्ष्मयोगेनैकीकृत्य प्रवेशस्थितिव्युत्थानैर्मन्त्रान्न्यसेदिति *चतुर्थं तत्त्वदर्शनम् ॥

इदानीं मन्त्रावधारणमन्त्रो लिख्यते — वज्रधृक् । हूं। ओं सुम्भ निसुम्भ हूं गृह्ण गृह्ण हूं G6 गृह्णापय गृह्णापय हूं आनय हो भगवन् विद्याराज

---

5 °āvadhārana<ṃ> em. : °āvadhāraṇa G **6** vyavastholi<s> em. : vyavastholi G **8** mantrā° em. : at(r)ā° G **11** nirūpita<ṃ> em. : nirūpita G **12** (sūkṣma)° G ○ caturtha(ṃn^{0}) G

हूं फट् । ओं घ ४ घातय घातय* सर्वदुष्टान् फट् २ कीलय २ सर्व-पापान् फट् २ हूं २ वज्रकील वज्रधरो आज्ञापयति सर्व G7 विघ्नानां काय-वाक्चित्तवज्रं* कीलय २ हूं २ फट् २ । टक्कि हूं जः । हूं । भ्रूं । ओं आः हूं । अनेन रक्षाचक्रालम्बनम्* ॥

अभावे भावनाऽभावो भावना नैव भावना ।
इति भावो* न G8 भावः स्याद्भावना नोपलभ्यते ॥

निःस्वभावालम्बनम् ॥

हूं यं हूं । हूं रं हूं । हूं वं हूं ।हूं लं हूं । चतुर्मण्डलनिष्पादनम् ॥

भ्रूं । कूटागारनिष्पादनम्* ॥

ओं शून्यताज्ञानवज्रस्वभावात्मको ऽहम् । परमार्थमण्डलप्रवेशः G9 ॥

सूर्यचन्द्रपद्मं च त्र्यक्षरवालं च । पर्यन्ते चन्द्रमण्डलालम्बनम् ॥

ओं धर्मधातुस्वभावात्मको ऽहम् । दृढीकरणम् । इति योगः ॥

ओं आः हूं । महावज्रधरनिष्पादनम्* । अनुयोगः ॥

ओं आः हूं स्वा हा । पञ्चस्कन्धानुप्रवेशः ॥

G28a G1 मोहरति द्वेषरति रागरति वज्ररति । धात्वनुप्रवेशः ॥

थ्लीं ओं ओं ओं हूं ओं सं मैं । चक्षुराद्यायतनानुप्रवेशः ॥

---

1 ghātaya ghātaya em. : ghātaka 2 ghātaya G **3** °vajra(ṃ) G
4 °cakrā⁻lambanaṃ G **6** bhāvo em. : bhāvye G **9** °niḥpādanaṃ G
13 °niḥṣpādanam G

हूं। यमान्तक-प्रज्ञान्तक-पद्मान्तक-अमृतकुण्डलि-अचल-टक्किराज-नीलदण्ड-महाबल-[G2]उष्णीषचक्रवर्ति*-निसुम्भराजश्चेति स्वकायमण्डल-निष्पादितस्वभावालम्बनं चेति। अतियोगः॥

ओं। अने*न लोचनाव्यूहस्फरणं॥

बुद्धकायधरः श्रीमांस्त्रिवज्राभेद्यभावितः।
अधिष्ठानपदं मे ऽद्य [G3]करोतु कायवज्रिणः॥

दशदिक्संस्थिता बुद्धास्त्रिवज्राभेद्यभाविताः।
अधिष्ठानपदं मे ऽद्य कुर्वन्तु कायवज्रिणः॥

अनेन प्रार्थना॥

यत्कायं सर्वबुद्धानां पञ्चस्कन्धप्रपूरितम्।
बुद्ध[G4]कायस्वभावेन ममापि तादृशं भवेत्॥

ओं सर्वतथागतकायवज्रस्वभावात्मको ऽहम्। अनेन कायवज्राधिष्ठानम्॥

आः। पाण्डरवासिनीव्यूहस्फरणम्॥

3 °varti° em. : °varttī G **5** (ane)na G

धर्मो वै वाक्पथः श्रीमांस्त्रिवज्राभेG5द्यभावितः ।
अधिष्ठानपदं मे ऽद्य करोतु वाग्वज्रिणः ॥

दशदिक्संस्थिता बुद्धास्त्रिवज्राभेद्यभाविताः ।
अधिष्ठानपदं मे ऽद्य कुर्व*न्तु वाग्वज्रिणः ॥

अनेन प्रार्थना ॥

यदे*व वज्रधG6र्मस्य वाचा निरुक्तिसम्पदा ।
ममापि तादृशी वाचा भवेद्धर्मधरोपमा* ॥

ओं सर्वतथागतवाग्वज्रस्वभावात्मको ऽहम् । अनेन वाग्वज्राहङ्कारं कुर्यादिति वाग्वज्राधिष्ठानम् ॥

हूं । मामकीव्यूहG7स्फरणम् ॥

चित्तवज्रधरः श्रीमांस्त्रिवज्राभेद्यभावितः ।
अधिष्ठानपदं मे ऽद्य करोतु चित्तवज्रिणः ॥

दशदिक्संस्थिता बुद्धास्त्रिवज्राभेद्यभाविताः ।
अधिष्ठानपदं मे ऽद्य कुर्वन्तु G8 चित्तवज्रिणः ॥

अनेन प्रार्थना ॥

4 kurva{¨}ntu G **6** eva em. : evaṃ G **7** °opamā em. : °opamāḥ G

यच्चित्तं समन्तभद्रस्य गुह्यकेन्द्रस्य धीमतः ।
ममापि तादृशं चित्तं भवेद्वज्रधरोपमम् ॥

ओं सर्वतथागतचित्तवज्रस्वभावात्मको ऽहम् । अनेन चित्तवज्राहङ्कारं कुर्यादिति चित्तवज्राधिष्ठानम् ॥ G9

ओं सर्वतथागतकायवाक्चित्तवज्रस्वभावात्मको ऽहम् । अनेन महावज्रधराहङ्कारं कुर्यादिति ॥

हूं । अनेन समाधिसत्वालम्बनम् ॥

एवं त्रिसत्वात्मकं महावज्रधरमात्मानं निष्पाद्य देवतीसंस्कारं कुर्यात् । G28b G1 अनेन क्रमेण — ओं आः हूं स्वा हा । लोचना मामकी पाण्डरवासिनी समयतारा । रूपवज्रा शब्दवज्रा गन्धवज्रा रसवज्रा स्पर्शवज्रा । वज्रवेताली* अपराजिता भृकुटी विश्ववज्री विश्वरत्नी विश्वपद्मी विश्वकर्मी G2 गगनवज्रिणी धरणींधरी* चेति प्राकृतस्त्रीभावापनयनम् ॥

ओं हूं । वज्रसंस्कारः ॥

आः । पद्मसंस्कारः ॥

ओं सर्वतथागतानुरागणवज्रस्वभावात्मको ऽहम् । रत्नसम्भवाधिष्ठानम् ॥

हूं । चालनं ॥

11 °vetālī em. : °vettālī G **12** dharaṇī<n>dharī em.

फट् । उत्सर्गः ॥

ओं सर्वतथागतपूजावज्र[G3]स्वभावात्मको ऽहम् । अमोघसिद्ध्यधिष्ठानम् ॥

उत्सर्गमण्डलस्य मन्त्रपदानि भवन्ति — वज्रधृक्' जिनजिक्' रत्नधृक्' आरोलिक्' प्रज्ञाधृक्' मोहरति' द्वेषरति' रागरति' वज्ररति' रूपवज्रा' शब्दवज्रा' [G4]गन्धवज्रा' रसवज्रा' स्पर्शवज्रा' मैत्रेयः*' क्षितिगर्भः' वज्रपाणिः' खगर्भः' लोकेश्वरः' मञ्जुश्रीः' सर्वनिवरणविष्कम्भी' समन्तभद्रः' यमान्तकृत्' प्रज्ञान्तकृत्' पद्मान्तकृत्' विघ्नान्तकृत्' अचलः' टक्किराजः' नीलदण्डः' महाबलः' उष्णीषचक्रवर्ती' सुम्भराजश्*[G5]चेत्युत्सर्गमण्डलम् ॥

सू*क्ष्मयोगः ॥

ओं आः हूं । वाग्जापः ॥

त्वं वज्रचित्त भुवनेश्वर सत्त्वधातो*
त्रायाहि मां रतिमनोज्ञ म[G6]हार्थकामैः ।
कामाहि मां जनक सत्त्वमहाग्रबन्धो
यदीच्छसे जीवितुमद्य* नाथ ॥

त्वं वज्रकाय बहुसत्त्वप्रियाङ्कचक्र
बुद्धार्थ बोधिपरमार्थ हितानुदर्शी ।

---

7 maitreya<ḥ> em. : maitreya G **10** °rāj{ā}aś G **11** sūkṣma° em. : śūkṣma° G **13** °dhāto em. : °dhātos G **16** jīvitum adya em. : jīvitu mahya G

रागेण रागसमयां मम कामयस्व
यदीच्छसे* [G7] जीवितुमद्य* नाथ ॥

त्वं वज्रवाच सकलस्य हितानुकम्पी
लोकार्थकार्यकरणे सद सम्प्रवृत्तः ।
कामाहि मां सुरतचर्य समन्तभद्र
यदीच्छसे जीवितुमद्य* नाथ ॥

त्वं वज्रकाम [G8] समयाग्र महाहितार्थ
सम्बुद्धवंशतिलक समतानुकम्पी
कामाहि मां गुननिधिं बहुरत्नभूतां
यदीच्छसे जीवितुमद्य* नाथ ॥

परमार्थप्रविष्टस्य सञ्चोदना ॥

अक्षोभ्यवज्र महाज्ञान वज्रधातु महाबुध ।
त्रिमण्डल त्रिवज्राग्रि भाष [G9] गुह्यं* नमो ऽस्तु ते ॥

वैरोचन महाशुद्ध वज्रशान्त महारते ।
प्रकृतिप्रभास्वरान्*धर्मान्देश वज्र नमो ऽस्तु ते ॥

2 yadīcchase em. : yadīcchase pa! G ○ jīvitum adya em. : jīvitu mahya G **6** jīvitum adya em. : jīvitu mahya G **10** jīvitum adya em. : jīvitu mahya G **13** bhāṣa guhyaṃ em. : bhāsa guhya G **15** °prabhāsvarān em. : °prabhāśvarān* G

रत्नराज सुगाम्भीर्य खवज्राकाशनिर्मल*।
G29a स्वभावशुद्ध निर्लेप (G1) भाष गुह्यं* नमो ऽस्तु ते ॥

वज्रामित महाराज निर्विकल्प खवज्रिणः ।
रागपारमिताप्राप्त भाष* वज्र नमो ऽस्तु ते ॥

अमोघवज्र सम्बुद्ध* सर्वाशापरिपूरक ।
शुद्धस्वभावसम्भूत वज्रसत्व नमो ऽस्तु ते ॥

पूर्वप्रणिधानवशाद्व्युत्थितस्य (G2) स्तुतिकरणम् ॥

हूं ॥ अनेन मन्त्रोपसंहारः ॥

इति श्रीगुह्यसमाजमहायोगतन्त्रे भवोत्पत्तिक्रमसाधनस्य मन्त्रोद्धारः समाप्तः ॥ कृतिरियं चन्द्रकीर्तिपादानाम् ॥ ॥

---

1 °nirmala em. : °nirmalaḥ G **2** bhāṣa guhyaṃ em. : bhāsa guhya G
4 bhāṣa em. : bhāsa G **5** sambuddha em. : sambhūta G

Bibliography

Bibliography

BANDURSKI 1994

FRANK BANDURSKI, Übersicht über die Göttinger Sammlungen der von RĀHULA SĀṄKṚTYĀYANA in Tibet aufgefundenen buddhistischen Sanskrit-Texte (Funde buddhistischer Sanskrit-Handschriften, III), Heinz BECHERT (ed.) *Sanskrit-Wörterbuch der buddhistischen Texte aus dem Turfan-Funden*, Beiheft 5, Göttingen: Vandenhoeck & Ruprecht 1994, pp. 9-126.

BENDALL 1883

CECIL BENDALL, *Catalogue of the Buddhist Sanskrit Manuscripts in the University Library, Cambridge* [reprint Stuttgart: Franz Steiner Verlag 1992].

CHAKRAVARTI 1984

CHINTAHARAN CHAKRAVARTI (ed.), *Guhyasamājatantrapradīpodyotanaṭīkāṣatkoṭivyākhyā*, Tibetan Sanskrit Works Series 25, Patna: Kashi Prasad Jayaswal Research Institute 1984.

DIKSHIT 1976

R. K. DIKSHIT, *Candellas of Jejākabhukti*, New Delhi: Abhinav Publications 1976.

HU-VON HINÜBER 2006

HAIYAN HU-VON HINÜBER, Some Remarks on the Sanskrit Manuscript of the Mūlasarvāstivāda-Prātimokṣasūtra from Tibet, *Jaina-Itihāsa-Ratna. Festschrift für Gustav Roth zum 90. Geburtstag*, Indica et Tibetica 47, Marburg: Indica et Tibetica Verlag 2006, pp. 283–337.

JIANG AND TOMABECHI 1996

JIANG ZHONGXIN and TOMABECHI TORU (eds.), *The Pañcakramaṭippaṇī of Muniśrībhadra. Introduction and Romanized Sanskrit Text*, Schweizer Asiatische Studien / Études asiatiques suisses, Monographien / Monographies 23, Bern: Peter Lang 1996.

KANO 2005

KANO KAZUO, Two Folios from Sthiramati's Triṃśikābhāṣya in Sanskrit Photographed by Rāhula Sāṅkṛtyāyana: Diplomatic and Critical Editions of Göttingen Xc 14/1e. *Wiener Zeitschrift für die Kunde Sudasiens* XLIX, 2005, pp. 113-149.

MATSUNAGA 1978

MATSUNAGA YŪKEI (ed.), *The Guhyasamājatantra*, Osaka: Toho Shuppan 1978.

MIMAKI AND TOMABECHI 1994

MIMAKI KATSUMI and TOMABECHI TORU, *Pañcakrama. Sanskrit and Tibetan Texts Critically Edited with Verse Index and Facimile Edition of the Sanskrit Manuscripts*, Bibliotheca Codicum Asiaticorum 8, Tokyo: The Center for East Asian Cultural Studies for Unesco 1994.

SALOMON 1998

RICHARD SALOMON, *Indian Epigraphy, A Guide to the Study of Inscriptions in Sanskrit, Prakrit, and the other Indo-Aryan Languages*, New Delhi: Munshiram Manoharlal Publishers Pvt. Ltd. 1998.

SANDERSON 2009

ALEXIS SANDERSON, The Śaiva Age — The Rise and Dominance of Śaivism During the Early Medieval Period—, Shingo EINOO (ed.) *Genesis and Development of Tantrism*, Tokyo: Institute of Oriental Culture, University of Tokyo 2009, pp. 41–349.

SĀṄKṚTYĀYANA 1935
RĀHULA SĀṄKṚTYĀYANA, Sanskrit Palm-leaf Mss. in Tibet, *Journal of the Bihar and Orissa Research Society* 21-1, 1935, pp. 21–43.

SĀṄKṚTYĀYANA 1938
RĀHULA SĀṄKṚTYĀYANA, Search for Sanskrit Mss. in Tibet, *Journal of the Bihar and Orissa Research Society* 24-4, 1938, pp. 137–163.

STEINKELLNER 1988
ERNST STEINKELLNER, Methodological Remarks on the Constitution of Sanskrit Texts from the Buddhist *Pramāṇa* Tradition, *Wiener Zeitschrift für die Kunde Südasiens* XXXII, 1988, pp. 103–129.

STEINKELLNER 2004
ERNST STEINKELLNER, *A Tale of Leaves. On Sanskrit manuscripts in Tibet, their Past and their Future*, 2003 Gonda Lecture, Amsterdam: Royal Netherlands Academy of Arts and Sciences 2004.

STEINKELLNER 2007
ERNST STEINKELLNER (ed.), *Dharmakīrti's Pramāṇaviniścaya. Chapters 1 and 2*, Sanskrit Texts from the Tibetan Autonomous Region No. 2, Beijing: China Tibetology Publishing House / Vienna: Austrian Academy of Sciences Press 2007.

TOMABECHI 2004
TOMABECHI TORU, Iwayuru *Vajrācāryanayottama* ni tsuite—Shinshutsu Kanrenshahon no Shōkai— (On the So-called *Vajrācāryanayottama*— Sanskrit Manuscript of a Related Text), *The Mikkyō Zuzō* (*The Journal of Buddhist Iconography*) 23, 2004, pp. 40–50.

TOMABECHI 2006
TOMABECHI TORU, *Étude du Pañcakrama. Introduction*

et Traduction annotée, Thèse de doctorat présentée à la Faculté des Lettres, Université de Lausanne, Lausanne: Université de Lausanne 2006.

TOMABECHI 2008
TOMABECHI TORU, Vitapāda, Śākyamitra, and Āryadeva: On a Transitional Stage in the History of *Guhyasamāja* Exegesis, *Esoteric Buddhist Studies: Identity in Diversity. Proceedings of the International Conference on Esoteric Buddhist Studies, Koyasan University, 5 Sept.–8 Sept. 2006*, Koyasan: Koyasan University 2008, pp. 171–177.

TRIPATHI 2001
RAM SHANKAR TRIPATHI (ed.), *Piṇḍīkrama and Pañcakrama of Ācārya Nāgārjuna*, Bibliotheca Indo-Tibetica Series 25, Sarnath-Varanasi: Central Institute of Higher Tibetan Studies 2001.

TRIPATHI AND NEGI 2001
RAM SHANKAR TRIPATHI and THAKUR SAIN NEGI (eds.), *Hevajratantram with Muktāvalī Pañjikā of Mahāpaṇḍitācārya Ratnākaraśānti*, Bibliotheca Indo-Tibetica Series 48, Sarnath-Varanasi: Central Institute of Higher Tibetan Studies 2001.

WAYMAN 1984
ALEX WAYMAN, The Sarvarahasyatantra, *Shinpi Shisō Ronshū*, Narita: Naritasan Shinshōji 1984, pp. 521–569.

WEDEMEYER 2007
CHRISTIAN K. WEDEMEYER, *Āryadeva's Lamp that Integrates the Practices. Caryāmēlāpakapradīpa. The Gradual Path of Vajrayāna Buddhism According to the Esoteric Community Noble Tradition*, New York: The American Institute of Buddhist Studies at Columbia University 2007.

图书在版编目（CIP）数据

月称《金刚萨埵成就法》：梵文、藏文、英文/罗鸿、苫米地等流校注.—北京：中国藏学出版社，2009.12
(西藏自治区梵文文本系列丛书)
ISBN 978-7-80253-207-6

Ⅰ.①月… Ⅱ.①罗…②苫… Ⅲ.大乘—佛经—研究—梵语、藏语、英文 Ⅳ.①B942.1

中国版本图书馆CIP数据核字(2009)第215241号

月称《金刚萨埵成就法》（梵文、藏文、英文）

出版：中国藏学出版社
发行：中国藏学出版社
责任编辑：南加才让
封面设计：李建雄
印刷：北京隆昌伟业印刷有限公司
开本：787×1092　1/16
印张：8.375
印次：2009年12月第1版第1次
印数：1000
书号：ISBN 978-7-80253-207-6/B · 82
定价：21.00元